"A Few Things I've Learned Since I Knew It All"

Other Books by

JERRY COOK
Choosing to Love (with Barbara Cook)
Love, Acceptance, and Forgiveness (with Stanley C. Baldwin)

STANLEY C. BALDWIN
Take This Job and Love It
The Overflowing Life
When Death Means Life
Bruised But Not Broken
How to Build Your Christian Character
A True View of You
Love, Acceptance, and Forgiveness (with Jerry Cook)
Your Money Matters (with Malcolm MacGregor)
What Makes You So Special?
What Did Jesus Say about That?
The Kink and I (with James Mallory)

"A Few Things I've Learned Since I Knew It All"

JERRY COOK

WITH STANLEY C. BALDWIN

WORD PUBLISHING

Dallas · London · Sydney · Singapore

Library of Congress Cataloging in Publication Data

Cook, Jerry.
    A few things I've learned since I knew it all / Jerry Cook with Stanley C. Baldwin.
        p.   cm.

    1. Theology.   2. Christian life—1960–   3. Cook, Jerry.
I. Baldwin, Stanley C.   II. Title.
BT77.C746   1989
230—dc19   89-5518
                                                                              CIP

ISBN 0–8499–0679–2

9 8 0 1 2 3 9   BKC   9 8 7 6 5 4 3 2 1
Printed in the United States of America

To Milton and LaVerne Cook

Through all the transitions of my life
They have been my cheering section

No son more loved than I
No parents more loved than they

Contents

CONTENTS

Part 1

A Few Things I've Learned about Myself

1

About Myself

I knew beyond all doubt that something was *very* wrong with me the day I entered my office and couldn't decide which chair to occupy.

I was the executive type, someone for whom big decisions came relatively easily. I was a successful pastor who had taken a church of twenty-three members and built it to forty-five hundred. "I dream big dreams, set directions, make far-reaching decisions," I had written. Now I stood paralyzed over the inconsequential choice of which chair to take, the one behind my desk or one of the three at my work table. It was ridiculous.

Summoning huge stores of inner strength and calling on all my coping mechanisms, I "ordered" myself to choose a chair. But I just couldn't do it. In frustration, I began to sob like a baby.

As if that weren't humiliating enough, Karen, my personal secretary, chose just that moment to enter through a door I thought I had locked. She caught me in the act of being insane.

"Are you OK?" she asked. She showed neither shock nor panic, just honest concern. Somehow her willingness to accept my weakness rather than run away enabled me to face myself. My anger and disappointment in not yet being well, three months after returning to work from heart surgery, gave way, and I reached out for help.

"No," I said, "I'm not OK. I feel like I'm losing my mind."

During the next hours, I was shuffled from one helping professional to another. What does one do with a pastor, someone responsible for a large suburban church, who can't figure out where to sit in his own office?

One of the people who helped answer that question was Dr. Joyce Dennison, a close friend and associate. I needed someone to step in and take decisive action. Joyce took up where my family doctor left off and put me in touch with Dr. Agatha Breckenridge. She was the first psychopharmacologist I had ever met—in fact, the first of which I had ever heard. "A physiological basis . . . a chemical imbalance." The phrases were encouraging, but this whole emotional thing was so hard for me to deal with. A voice kept telling me, "Christians don't have emotional problems, you know."

It appeared that there might be some specific, physical explanation for my worsening depression and sense of incompetence. There was a lot of guesswork, too—"chemical imbalance due to prolonged and severe stress—possibly some damage due to lack of oxygen during the heart attack or surgery." It sounded pretty vague, all except for Dr. Breckenridge's prescription. "Reverend Cook, I want you out of town by Friday."

No one called me "Reverend Cook." I thought, "I must be worse off than I imagined!"

And so it was. I was "out of town by Friday" to a chalet some 9,000 feet high in the Colorado Rockies. This was where I was to get well.

WHAT HAPPENED TO JERRY COOK?

There were tears and hugs when I left, of course, and brave promises that we would all be together again soon—

and secret doubts in many hearts, mine included, that the
old Jerry Cook would ever return.

My wife, Barb, and I agreed that she would stay behind
and do what she could to maintain a normal home for
our children. My dad drove me to Colorado, and we took
the scenic route. Actually, we stretched a two-day,
one-thousand-mile trip into a relaxed and wandering
eight-day, three-thousand-mile journey. It was a sort of
pretending that everything was all right and that our trip
was purely for fun.

But we did finally get there, and then Dad left, and I was
alone. I stood feeling hollow and desolate in this beautiful
and strange place that I already loved a little and hated a
little. Dad was on his way home. I hoped that, in another
sense, I was too.

What a new and curious feeling this was! There was no
place I had to be soon. No telephone invaded my life to
demand something from me. I had no meetings to attend
or sermons to prepare. It was as though all that had ceased
to exist, and I suspected that I had ceased to exist with it.

I was no longer the familiar and comfortable "Pastor"
or "Jerry" I had been, nor even the strange-sounding
"Reverend Cook." Oh, my therapist would call me Jerry,
but I wouldn't be a person he would look to for leadership
and spiritual guidance. I'd be his patient, not his pastor. I
wouldn't be anybody's pastor.

If I wasn't anybody's pastor, who or what was I?

"You're a mess, Jerry, but we can help you." Dr. Hazel
Goddard sat calmly, looking into me. Twenty years of psy-
chiatric practice in South Chicago had convinced her that
the healing of her patients could best be accomplished
here in these magnificent Colorado mountains. She had
established her practice here and had treated various
Christian leaders and others. Now she sat there telling
me what I was—a mess.

Dr. Goddard's unflattering observation about my condition had nowhere near as much impact as her words of hope. *We can help you.* How intensely I wanted her to be right. I wanted it so much that I was overwhelmed, and the tears, never far away now, rushed to my eyes again.

About all I did those first days in Colorado was to sit and feel and listen to the loneliness. Later came reading, sketching, some writing, and lots of reflection. A good deal of that reflection focused on a subject of more than passing interest to me: *Whatever happened to Jerry Cook?*

It's clear now, in retrospect, that what happened to Jerry Cook was complex. No simple answers can explain it all. No one thing, done differently, would have saved the day. Simply put, I was an organism out of order, an organism that had shut down for a while in order to survive.

THE BOY IN THE BOX

One thing that had exacted a heavy toll on me was the stress of living by a win/lose mentality. The subtle power of that mentality is illustrated by a frightening news story I read some time ago involving a boy just six or seven years old. It all started when he was taken from his mother at the age of one because she was a drug addict.

The boy was placed in the custody of a stepmother, and she kept him in a box two feet wide, two feet high, and six feet long. He lived in this box—not for a day or for a week—for years. He was taken out on Sundays, if you can imagine that, and driven to Sunday school. He was also taken out to go to the bathroom. Every time, however, he was returned to the box.

One of the most terrifying things about the whole ugly business was that the child believed that all children lived in boxes. What "is" tends to become "normal." I don't know if that child can ever be recovered. How do you take that

14

kind of warpage out of a person's life? It requires a miracle of God.

Tragic as his story is and bizarre as it may seem, the truth is that the boy in the box is you and the boy in the box is me. Despite our protests to the contrary, the unpleasant fact is that from infancy we have been raised in a box. We have grown up in a distorted and fallen world even though we may have gone to Sunday school periodically. The irony is that we don't even know how things should be. For us, as for the boy in the box, what "is" has become "normal."

The world, our stepmother, has done horrible things to us, and we have allowed her to warp us because we believed that we had no other option.

THE WIN/LOSE MENTALITY

The box in which you and I grew up exalts winning and despises losing. The secular culture constantly feeds us that viewpoint. Sports figures, if they can keep winning, are paid outrageous sums of money. It has gotten to the point that the president of the most powerful nation on earth is paid $200,000 a year, but someone who can beat a rival senseless for the heavyweight boxing championship might collect millions of dollars for that single fight.

Vince Lombardi, the legendary Green Bay Packers coach, stated it succinctly: "Winning isn't the main thing; it's the only thing."

Not only did the society in which I grew up worship winning, but so, too often, did the church. I can't tell you how many conference banners have proclaimed "Winning with Jesus," how many seminars have promised that "God makes winners out of losers," how many books have declared that they can show me "How to Win in Life."

Once in a while I was taken out of my box to catch

glimpses of a different world. I remember Alex, for example. I met Alex my first Sunday as pastor at East Hill. He was carried into the sanctuary and carefully placed on the front bench by Everett, a big, rawboned outdoorsman. Alex was desperately crippled. He couldn't control either his arms or his legs. He couldn't talk well. In fact, it was some time before I could understand him at all.

When I got to know Alex, I discovered he had a keen mind and a wonderful sense of humor. We grew to love each other. His home was the County Farm, a wretched, smelly place that the county finally closed, leaving Alex without a home. He ended up in a rest home that agreed to accept his welfare check in exchange for room and board.

Alex was not and would never be a winner. He would never own more than he could stuff in a paper sack. Win? Alex couldn't even compete. The general community, those few who ever saw him, either ignored or patronized him.

Yet I knew beyond a shadow of a doubt that Alex was somebody.

There were others like Alex over the years. Danny is a Down-syndrome child. Whenever he sees me, he breaks loose and runs to me. He always does three things. He grins and calls my name; he gives me a hug; he happily shows me his new watch. Danny has worn that watch for at least two years, but it is brand new to us every time we meet, and we spend a little time raving about it.

Don't mention winners and losers when you talk about Danny. The concept is both irrelevant and repugnant. To reduce Danny to a commodity, to judge him by his performance, is obscene.

It's clear to me now that judging anyone by performance and by comparison with others is profane. Why should Alex or Danny be any different? Because they are handicapped? If so, we all meet the qualifications; we are all

handicapped. I have yet to meet a flawless person or anyone who comes near perfection.

For most of my life, however, I haven't adequately understood that. Perhaps I have assented to it intellectually,
but I haven't been able to accept it for my own life. A few
glimpses of another value system aren't enough to free one
from years in the box. Not when the winning-is-every-
thing myth so dominates us that we are intimidated even
to question it.

Go ahead and raise the issue. Suggest that winning isn't
really that important. What happens immediately? "You're
just a sore loser," one hears whispered from somewhere
close-by: "You don't have any trophies in your case. . . .
You've never tasted the thrill of victory. . . . You've
never been on the winning team."

In order to respond, I have to catalog my victories, to
prove the accusing voice wrong by showing that I am a
winner. But that is exactly what I'm protesting. Why do I
have to prove I am somebody by listing my triumphs? Why
must I win in order to validate my existence? If I try to
prove that I really am a winner "in my own way," I'm right
back in the box.

I lived there too long. It was home to me for too long.

A telling entry in my journal, dated three months before
I left for Colorado, reads as follows: "I think I try to change
everything to a win/lose and go for the win. There is a
high cost for winning and a high cost for losing. Sadly, I
don't know another way to live."

THE BUSY/IMPORTANT/SERIOUS SYNDROME

The win/lose mentality produced in me a certain
grimness that I call the Busy/Important/Serious syn-
drome. Busy, important, and serious hang out together,
and they take over the lives of winners.

Surely you've noticed this. Important people are always

busy. They rush from somewhere to somewhere else.
Wherever they are is typically on the way to where they
are going, to some destination that is never quite clear but
always more important than here.

It is all very seductive. I am busy because I am important, and I am important because I am busy. It has a certain
rush, an intoxication, an excitement. Researchers report
that we can actually get high on and become addicted to
our own adrenalin. Living on an adrenalin high, however,
leaves me weary, but I don't read that as a warning from
my body that something is amiss. Instead, I read my
weariness as evidence of heroism; it shows how dedicated
I am to Christ and to the work of Christ.

"I'm so tired," I say to myself, "but I must keep going. I
am important, needed." I'm also deliciously aware that
others are saying with admiration, "He works so hard.
How can he possibly accomplish so much. He certainly is
a great man of God."

I hear bits and pieces of this, translate it into more evidence of my importance, and slide closer and closer to the
precipice. All the while, I think things are as they should
be; that's the way my box is.

Then comes the crash. It can take various forms—a
body gone on strike, emotions no longer reflecting reality,
a marriage in trouble. Now winners hang on the brink of
becoming—horror of horrors—losers. "He is certainly a
great man of God," is replaced with, "If he were really
a man of faith, how could this happen?" Or, "There must
have been some hidden sin in his life."

Hidden failings could be responsible, of course, but it's
also possible that they've just succumbed to overload,
to the seductive power of Busy/Important/Serious and to
fatigue.

The fatigue I'm talking about has little to do with taking
a day off now and then or going for a long walk on the

beach. There is a tiredness those little respites won't touch.
It's the bone-weariness of a never-ending competition that
God never called us to enter in the first place. A tiredness
whose companions are Busy/Important/Serious.

Oh, yes, Serious is the third partner in this devastating
and seductive little trio. Like a virus, Serious infected my
entire being. Fun and spontaneity and life and laughter,
feeling unwanted and unwelcome, slipped quietly away.

The precious things tiptoed out of my life lest they dis-
tract this busy and important man from doing God's serious business. In Colorado, I began to realize how long they
had been gone and how much I missed them. After a
while, I tried to write about it to Barb.

> Laughter,
>> Not strained or shallow.
>> Fun laughter, it just sort of bubbles out, easy,
>> smooth.
> The kind that people have when they are enjoying
> Not anything in particular, everything in general.
>> A being-together kind of laughter.
> Somewhere . . . sometime . . . somehow,
>> I traded "being" laughter for "doing" laughter.
>
> "Doing" laughter is OK.
>> It's real and fun and . . .
>> Somehow, it's not enough.
> At least, not enough between companions.
> "Doing" laughter seems to wear out.
>> It's always looking for another event,
> Something to liberate it for another brief moment,
>> Only to be abandoned in search of another.
>
> It is "being" laughter
>> That I am seeking with you, my Love.
>> Yet the search itself denies it;
> It is not something searched for.
> It is a sort of rushing, a surprise,

19

A serendipity of . . . fellowship.

Cartwheels on the sand,
   Imperfect, yet more beautiful than a dozen
gold-medal performances.
Singing,
   Not great but worth the London Symphony as
accompaniment.
Rides, Walks, Stolen kisses.
   Easy, smooth.
   There it was! "Being" laughter.

Then . . .
   I got serious.
   Life got serious.
   Demands, supposed omnipotence.
The universe surely required my involvement to survive!
And "being" laughter slipped away, like a shadow.
   It slipped past me
   And walked on with my baby girl
      (Fathering a perfect child is serious business).
   It walked on with my Love
      (Being head of the house and priest in the home
   and spiritual leader and final authority and . . .
   and . . .
   It's serious business, you know!)

And my children laughed,
   But not with me.
   "He's tired" . . . "He's sick" . . . "He's angry"
He's gone away, into his own lonely, serious world.
   A world of "doing" laughter,
   A world of objects and duties
   And calendars, (God curse them!)
   And things, problems, expectations.
   Airports, motels, conferences, jet lag,
      Endless introductions
And the children laughed as they grew
But I was doing important things, and missed them.

My Love laughed,
>But not with me.
"We must be serious in the presence of this great man
>about such magnificent things."

Where did this fellow come from?
>He's like being sentenced to carry a corpse for
penance.
>>"A mild heart attack," they said.
>>"An angiogram," they said, "just to be sure."
>>"Surgery," they said.
>>"Heart disease," they said.
And who is this fellow that is left?
He doesn't want to be serious, but what else is there?

Maybe, if given a chance, and help
>A person will emerge.
>A day will come,
>I'm not sure just how,
>When, without the corpse,
>My Love and I will laugh together again.
Laughter
>Not strained or shallow.
>"Being" laughter.
>It just sort of bubbles out.
>The kind of laughter people have
>When they are . . . enjoying.

God did free me from the tyranny of the win/lose mentality and restored me to "being" laughter with my family. In the next chapter, I'll tell you how.

2

More about Myself

How does a person who is caught up in a competitive, win/lose lifestyle get out of that box?

For me, it required a shattering experience, a descent into a dark night of the soul. I experienced depression and intense loneliness and great pain—virtually a visit to hell. The seeds of my recovery were sown in suffering.

I suppose this is typical. Dr. James D. Mallory writes in *The Kink and I:* "Most of us will not change unless we are hurting in some way emotionally. . . . C. S. Lewis, in a profound book called *The Problem of Pain,* states that God whispers to us in our joys and shouts to us in our pain. Very often, that is true; and we don't hear until he shouts."

God was shouting to me there in Colorado. I can see that clearly in retrospect. My poem to Barb, in which I cried in pain for the "being" laughter, was an attempt on my part to respond to God's shout.

Even my earlier, despairing journal entry contained a hidden element of hope: "I try to change everything to a win/lose and go for the win. . . . Sadly, I don't know another way to live." There was a seed of recovery in that; I at least was recognizing that my condition was sad. No longer did the boy in the box believe his situation to be right and normal. So, then, just as the seeds of disaster were growing in my life when I was on top—an active, successful, even "heroic" pastor—so the seeds of recovery were beginning to grow when I was at the bottom.

I was beginning to learn another way to live. My hope is that others can learn something from my experience. That is why I have described my pain and now want to describe some of the insights that I have gained.

WINNING AS IT IS JUDGED BY GRACE

I may have given you the impression that I am totally opposed to winning and to competition of any kind. That may bother some readers who are aware that the Bible speaks favorably of winning. For example, Paul writes, "Do you not know that in a race all the runners run, but only one gets the prize? Run in such a way as to get the prize" (1 Cor. 9:24).

There is such a thing as appropriate competition and there is appropriate winning. We can distinguish between healthy and unhealthy competition if we will bring competition under the judgment of those Christian values that we know to be both true and basic: *grace* and *love*.

Grace teaches us that we stand accepted before God apart from any meritorious works of our own. We need not and cannot perform in order to gain or keep a right standing with God. If we have trusted in Christ as Savior, God has put His perfect righteousness to our account. We are accepted in the Beloved—totally, completely accepted.

Nothing we do—no amount of winning—can improve our standing with God. To think so is to offend grace. Therefore, we must not try to make winning a base of our acceptance with God.

We can, however, seek to win our race based on the fact that we are already accepted by God. In other words,

winning is appropriate when it is *from* a base of acceptance with God and not *as* a base for such acceptance.

At this point some reader is certain to reply, "Well, of
course, I know I don't have to be a winner to be saved; I
am saved by grace, so I easily pass your test at that point."

I'm not so sure. Notice I spoke about "a base of acceptance with God" rather than about "the base of your salvation." Many a person who claims salvation by grace still
feels less than fully accepted by God.

A woman said to me, "If my prayers are to be heard
and answered by God, my heart has to be clean and my
motives pure." Although she phrased it as a statement, I
knew she was asking for my observation on that particular
viewpoint.

"Aren't you glad that's not true?" I replied with a smile.

Go ahead. Have a pure motive sometime. This I want to
see. Even our best actions are tainted with self-serving
and human frailty. The woman's attitude about prayer is
the kind of thinking that causes us to appeal to somebody
more holy to do our praying. We aren't pure enough, so we
ask a saint or a priest or a clergyman to pray for us. They
are the "winners" in the kingdom of the holy, and we are
the losers.

Thus the win/lose mentality paralyzes us spiritually
and even locks us out of prayer. It reminds me of a
preacher I once knew who came to such paralysis in
another arena: he couldn't choose which chair to occupy
in his own office.

WINNING AS JUDGED BY LOVE

The second great tenet of Christianity by which we must
judge winning and all forms of competition is love.

When I was trapped in win/lose, I was constantly
assessing my value on the basis of how well I stacked up
alongside someone else. If the comparison was favorable to

me, and it usually was, then all was well—for me. Someone else lost by virtue of the fact that I won, but I forgot to apply to winning and losing the words of Jesus about loving others as I love myself.

Whenever winning is inconsistent with love, it violates Christ's greatest commandment and offends the Lord. Scripture says we are to "spur one another on toward love and good deeds" (Heb. 10:24). Frankly, many Christians seem to think the only way they and others can be spurred to good works is by unloving competition, that is, by win/lose. I will work in order to outdo you or to look better than you. This Scripture, however, assumes that we can be motivated toward love *and* good works. We don't have to sacrifice one in favor of the other.

Too often, blind to the element of love so central to Christian faith, we baptize our unloving rivalry as something that honors God. Eventually, the ugly results begin to show themselves. A Baptist pastor, John Claypool, was also confined from childhood to the win/lose box. When Claypool was converted to Christ and even when he became a minister he retained his basic competitive mentality. He writes in *The Preaching Event:*

> I must say, also, that life in the parish ministry has not been a whole lot different. I can still recall going to state and national conventions in our denomination and coming home feeling drained and unclean, because most of the conversation in the hotel rooms and the halls was characterized either by envy of those who were doing well or scarcely concealed delight for those who were doing poorly. For did that not mean that someone was about to fall, and would thus create an opening higher up the ladder? . . .
>
> About ten years out of the seminary I began to feel a variety of disquieting emotions. For one thing, I was really bone-weary. Do you have any idea how much energy it takes always to have to succeed and come out number one? I was also beginning to sense

how lonely and isolated this way of living leaves one. How can you really relate openly and warmly to persons when you realize that at a deeper level you are competing with them and trying to outdo them?

So, then, winning is fine, just make sure it's not at the expense of grace or love. Keep it from assuming any role in your standing with God; that's all by grace. Keep it from damaging others or making you indifferent or superior; that's inconsistent with love.

Is anything left? Can we go for the win at all? Certainly, we can be "more than conquerors through him who loved us" (Rom. 8:37). We can win over hardship and adversity and danger and apathy. We can win over frustration by learning patience.

There is also a whole world of legitimate winning besides these personal inner victories. We can win over the dandelions in our yards and over the toilets that won't quit running and over the collection agency computers that try to collect debts we don't owe.

To help us turn away from the win/lose mentality that displeases God, I suggest the following:

1. We Must Accept Our Personal Uniqueness

When I had heart surgery, I asked one of the surgeons how long my recovery should take. He answered, "It should take as long as it takes." He went on to explain that my recovery was exactly that, *my* recovery, not someone else's. Each person's body is unique, each reacts differently to trauma, and each heals at its own pace. "Don't compare your progress with anybody else's," he told me, "and don't try to speed along your recovery as if you have some deadline to meet."

That was wise counsel. My tendency was to want to beat the norm. If the doctor had said that most people recover in six weeks, I'd have tried for five weeks or, better yet, five days! Then I would have given God the glory—supposedly. Actually, it would have been an ego boost for myself, another way to reassure myself that I am not ordinary, I am a "winner."

Watch out for this world's so-called norms. Often they are nothing but arbitrary standards for the game of win/lose. There is only one of you, so it is impossible to set a norm for how long it "should" take you to do something you haven't done previously.

2. We Must Separate Our Person from
Our Performance

In the previous chapter, I mentioned that a heavyweight fighter might receive millions of dollars for a single fight. Suppose such a person lost his right hand in an accident and could never fight again. He would then be unable to command huge sums of money for exploits in the ring. Question: Is he therefore any less worthwhile as a person? To phrase the question in another way, does this person's worth reside in his right hand?

Most people would agree that such an idea is absurd. If a person is a prize fighter, his value as a commodity certainly resides in his fists. His worth as a person, however, does not. So the question becomes one of whether we view ourselves and others as commodities or as persons. If we are commodities, performance (and winning) is everything. If we are persons, performance needs only to reflect capability, whether that capability is great or small.

Performance is dependent not only on our health and strength but also upon the opportunities that come our way. What about a young man who has all the physical requisites to be a world-champion heavyweight fighter but never has the opportunity to put on the gloves? Let's say our potential champion grew up in a culture that never heard of boxing. His strength and agility are devoted to working the soil instead of working over an opponent. Is he therefore less worthwhile as a person?

I had the opportunity to lead a suburban church in explosive growth. I also had the vigor to serve in that demanding ministry. The day came, however, when my stamina and strength were depleted. It became necessary for me to accept a secondary role, as associate pastor. My influence, status, and public position declined. Does that make me less worthwhile as a person?

Quite honestly, I had to deal with that question, and it took a while. I did feel less valuable as a person—but not any more. My new life has more "being" laughter as contrasted with the old "doing" laughter. In fact, my whole focus has switched from doing to being.

The theological basis for a life of being rather than doing was already in place. I had been preaching it for years. Jesus consistently taught it. "Make a tree good and its fruit will be good, or make a tree bad and its fruit will be bad. . . . For out of the overflow of the heart the mouth speaks" (Matt. 12:33–34). These are expressions of the crucial importance of what we are as a determinant of what we do and say.

Previously I had applied the principle of *being determines doing* as follows: I am a winner and, therefore, I must win. The only alternative I saw was to be a loser who, therefore, loses. Surely God didn't want me to be a loser.

The irrelevance of win/lose categories in describing my person hadn't yet dawned on me. But, thank God, a way of life not dominated by a win/lose mentality has emerged from the ashes of my old life. You might say it's something I've learned since I knew it all.

Part 2

A Few Things
I've Learned about
God

3

About God

A ll my life I have believed in a God who can and does
work miracles. Even a cursory reading of the Bible,
whether Old Testament or New, reveals the Lord to be a
God of miracles. Jesus came performing signs and wonders, and he offered these as evidence that he was sent
from God. The Apostles performed miracles in the name
of Christ. I myself have witnessed and experienced what I
consider to be miracles of divine intervention in human
sickness and tragedy.

THE GOD WHO SQUARES WITH REALITY

I also believe there is danger in conceiving of the "miracle-
working God" in such a way that we deny reality and distort God's true nature. (Whenever we deny reality, we
distort the nature of God, because he *is* ultimate reality.)

I witnessed some examples of denying reality in the
name of God in 1984 when I suffered a serious heart attack and subsequently underwent by-pass surgery. A man
came to visit me while I was recovering. I was still in con-
siderable pain. He asked me how I was feeling, and I made
the mistake of telling him. "I'm hurting quite a bit right
now," I said.

"Don't claim it, brother!" he sternly corrected me.

Claim it? I wasn't claiming it. I was *experiencing* it. When your heart is practically cut out and repaired, it hurts. It's supposed to hurt. My visitor thought, however, that one speaks such things as pain into existence and that I was giving it a reality it needn't have had.

Such thinking poses as superior spirituality, but it is based on ideas of God quite foreign to biblical truth. Most evangelicals recognize the error, even the absurdity, of Christian Science which denies the reality of matter and sin and sickness. Yet when some of the same ideas are couched in warm evangelical terms, many fall for them.

In my own case, my very real body recovered sufficiently from its very real illness for me to return to my pulpit. One Sunday a woman came up to talk to me. "Weren't you embarrassed to have a heart attack?" she asked.

I couldn't believe I had heard her right, so I asked her to say it again. She did, and I assured her that having a heart attack, bad as it was, had not been particularly embarrassing to me. As we talked further I realized that the embarrassment had been to her theology. She could not understand how a servant of the true and living God could have a heart attack. And I certainly should have had enough faith not to require surgery afterward!

Underlying this woman's attitude was an assumption about God—namely, that God would not allow serious illness to affect those who please him. I believe the Bible teaches otherwise. My own experience definitely testifies otherwise. Heart disease and all sorts of other illnesses afflict people of faith.

Why did I have a heart attack? A combination of circumstances caused it. Maybe some were genetic, some were behavioral, and some were unknown. The natural result of everything going on in my body led to a heart attack. God didn't send it. He also did not suspend natural law to prevent it, just as he did not keep the saints of old from dying when they were sawn asunder or burned at the stake.

Many others besides myself, of course, have experienced similar collisions of theology with reality. I met a young man who had lost both legs to a mine in Vietnam. He was in a wheelchair, naturally, and was an advocate for disabled veterans. We were talking, and he commented, "The person you least want to be in the world is a handicapped person in a charismatic church."

I said, "Why is that?"

"Well," he said, "for the first three or four weeks you're a project to prove their theology of healing. But if you're not healed [in his case, if he didn't grow legs], then you become an embarrassment to their theology, and they don't quite know what to do with you."

Granted, that was his experience and not reflective of all charismatic churches nor was his experience necessarily typical. Still, I must tell you that as he talked, something inside told me, "You need to listen; you need to learn something here." You see, I am deeply committed to the miraculous intervention of God in human sickness and tragedy, but my theology—my God, if you will—has to square with reality.

A TWISTED VIEW OF GOD LEADS TO A TWISTED LIFE

Our concept of God decisively affects the rest of our lives. Ultimately we become like whatever god we worship. This is the case whether we worship the true and living God or some gross distortion.

Psalm 115 depicts those who worship idols as follows: "But their idols are silver and gold, made by the hands of men. They have mouths, but cannot speak, eyes, but they cannot see; they have ears, but cannot hear, noses, but they cannot smell; they have hands, but cannot feel, feet, but they cannot walk; nor can they utter a sound with their throats. *Those who make them will be like them, and so will all who trust in them"* (vv. 4–8, emphasis added).

In the same way, those who worship the true God become like him. We read in 2 Corinthians: "And we, who with unveiled faces all contemplate the Lord's glory, are being transformed into his likeness with ever-increasing glory" (3:18, marginal reading).

James Michener, well-known author and novelist, in his book *The Source*, illustrates how people become like the god they worship. Like Michener's other books, *The Source* gives valuable information because the author does his homework well. He researches thoroughly the historical settings of his novels and then writes a fictional narrative accurately incorporating that data.

The Source is a story about life in and around ancient Palestine. It tells a story of a couple living in 2200 B.C., who, after many years, finally have a son, and they are thrilled about it. This occurs during a period when human sacrifices were offered to the god, Melak. When the couple's child is about nine months old, the priests warn the people that the stars indicate an imminent military threat from the north. In order to be sure Melak will protect them, the town must sacrifice eight firstborn sons to him.

So it is that the father, Urbaal, enters his house one day and finds red marks on his son's arms. His wife is distraught. The priests have come through and marked their son for sacrifice. Urbaal has to act as though this is wonderful; it is a privilege to be chosen by the god. Although his wife is in shock, Urbaal tells her not to weep or show any displeasure lest Melak be angry with them.

The huge stone idol of Melak has wide, flat arms outstretched. The arms form an inclined plane so that a child placed on them tumbles toward a gaping hole, which is the god's mouth. Inside, a roaring fire quickly consumes the sacrifice.

When the hour comes for the public sacrifice, the mother cannot bear to attend. She begs Urbaal to let her stay at home, but since that might suggest a "grudging" spirit on her part, her husband cannot allow it.

At the ceremony, one of the other mothers screams when her son is fed to the fire. The priests show their displeasure at this unseemly outburst, and Urbaal grips his wife by the arm and warns her to remain silent. When her own son is raised into the air and hurled upon the stone arms of death, the mother cannot control herself. She begins to cry out, but her husband's hand stifles her cries. Michener describes what is going on inside of her. You begin to feel what she is feeling as she loses her only child.

A bit later you read of her husband's yearning for a voluptuous temple priestess. Another aspect of their worship is temple prostitution, and Michener describes the rites and the seeming logic of this ancient fertility cult. As a part of it all, one especially productive farmer is selected to spend seven days cavorting with the beautiful priestess. Who will be chosen for this honor?

Urbaal presses forward with the others, the prayer "Let it be me!" on his lips. The priests announce their choice. It is Urbaal, and his wife watches as he gathers the nude priestess into his arms and disappears into the Hall of Astarte with her: "And while others celebrated she walked slowly homeward, seeing life in a new and painful clarity: with different gods her husband Urbaal would have been a different man."

When I read that, I just had to lay the book aside and say, "That is so true!" The kind of God we worship determines what kind of people we are and what behavior we approve.

KEEPING MELAK OUT OF CHRISTIANITY

You may be thinking how bizarre and hideous the ancient worship of Melak was. You may believe that nothing like that could happen today, at least not in civilized lands and not with the approval of society. You are right, of course, but some elements of what passes for Christian worship are uncomfortably similar to the worship of Melak. Perhaps an experience I had will help you understand what I mean.

A woman came to me and said, "I hate God! I will never serve him because I hate him."

"Why would you say such a thing?" I asked. "You don't want to say that. You're picking a terrible fight to take on God."

She said, "I hate God; he killed my baby."

I said, "God killed your baby? Tell me how he did it."

She described how her eighteen-month-old child had fallen victim to a freak fatal accident.

I said, "How is God responsible for that?"

She said, "At the funeral the preacher told everyone, 'The Lord giveth and the Lord taketh away. Blessed be the name of the Lord.' When I heard that, I determined that I would never serve a God who kills babies, and I never will."

I said, "My dear, I join you in that. I won't either. Would you be open to questioning that conclusion? Maybe it wasn't God who killed your baby."

I'm glad to report that she was willing to reconsider.

I believe it was a terrible misuse of that line from the Book of Job—"The Lord giveth and the Lord taketh away" —to apply it to the accidental death of a child. Think about it. Isn't a God who kills babies a great deal like Melak? Granted, the circumstances are different. This mother didn't watch her baby burn to death. Nevertheless, the basic concept of God is uncomfortably similar. For some ostensibly good end, he requires the life of an innocent child and devastates the mother.

Certainly God does bring good out of evil. He brought salvation for mankind out of the murder of Jesus. That is quite different from saying, however, that God does evil in order to bring about good. Paul condemns that kind of thinking as it applies to us (see Rom. 3:8 and 6:1–2). We are not to do evil that good may come, and neither does God.

Therefore, I do not believe that God kills babies. But here's the point: If I did believe God would do that sort of thing, it would have an effect on me. For one thing, I would be more likely to stifle a bereaved mother's grief, as Urbaal did his wife's, instead of weeping with her as the Scripture says I should.

Does God Have a Dark Side?

Our society, many Christians included, buys into the idea that God is personally responsible for everything bad that happens. There was an earthquake in California recently. Whose name will appear as the cause of all the damage on the insurance forms? It was "an act of God." Some homes in the area escaped severe damage. Why? "Those people were just lucky." Luck gets credit for the good things, and God gets the blame for the bad. That's the kind of goofy world we live in. What foolishness!

Do you have at least one good thing in your life right now? That is God's doing. The good things are from God. "Don't be deceived, my dear brothers. Every good and perfect gift is from above, coming down from the Father of the heavenly lights, who does not change like shifting shadows" (James 1:16–17).

Get that? God does not change. God does not have a shadowy, sinister side. I read an article recently about "the dark side of God." It cited Isa. 45:7 from the King James Version—"I form the light, and create darkness: I make peace, and create evil: I the Lord do all these things." The writer also quoted Prov. 16:4, "The Lord hath made all things for himself: yea, even the wicked for the day of evil." To use these passages to make God an agent of evil borders on blasphemy. Other translations give a different thrust. For example, the New International Version translates Prov. 16:4, "The Lord works out everything for his own ends—even the wicked for a day of disaster." The reader will recognize, I am sure, that it is quite different to say "God overrules evil to bring good" as contrasted with "God has a dark side that fosters evil for his own good purposes."

The Apostle James assures us in the passage cited above that God is symbolized by the warm, cheering, and life-giving sunlight, except sunlight changes. It gets bright in midday and disappears at night. God, however, is always the same—good. As the Apostle John states flatly, "God is light; in him there is no darkness at all" (1 John 1:5). So much for the supposed "dark side" of God.

You need to know this about God: he has no dark side. You especially need to know it when your life collapses around you, as mine did. Lying in the hospital, suffering, not knowing whether anything that was life to me would remain, I didn't need to wonder also about God's intentions toward me.

Victor Frankl was incarcerated in a concentration camp during World War II because he was Jewish. The foundation of his later work as a psychiatrist was germinated by this prison experience. Addressing the question of whether a doctor should ever pull the plug on a patient in a coma, Frankl says, "One thing we must guard as physicians, the person must know that we are coming to serve his life and his health and that we will never come as his executioner."

It's important that patients have that confidence in the medical profession, and it's also important that people have that confidence in their God. He will never come as our executioner.

Opposite Errors with Similar Results

Let's pause now to sum up what we have been saying. People truly do become like whatever God they worship. Our concept of God decisively affects all the rest of our lives. It is utterly crucial, then, that the God we worship and present to others be the one true and living God.

We have talked about two errors people make about God. The first is the belief that God will intervene to spare those who please him from the vicissitudes of life. That view does not square with reality. I suffered a devastating heart attack with all its attendant consequences. My amputee friend in the wheelchair did not grow new legs. No matter how godly a person may be, he will still be subject to physical decay, degeneration, and death. After all, not one of the original Apostles is around anymore!

The second error about God is the belief that he goes along with and even sponsors evil, that he shrugs at human suffering because it is a means to his ends. We have said that God does not kill babies or otherwise do evil so that good may come. He is a God of compassion and love, a God of light in whom there is no darkness at all.

I am a different and better person—and certainly a better witness—if I worship the God I have just described than I would be otherwise. For you see, whichever error of the two I make—whether I have a God who kills babies or a God who prevents all natural calamities for those who please him—I end up hurting people instead of helping them. If I present a baby-killing God, I alienate people because they rightly reject a God who is more monster than loving Father. By the opposite error, however, I cruelly insinuate that suffering people have offended a good God who would surely intervene to spare them if they weren't so desperately out of his will.

In these ways we too often sacrifice people on the altar of our theology. Like Urbaal we stifle their cries. Alas, if only we had a different God, we would be different people.

4

More about God

The cruelty of Christians who injure others—or themselves—in the name of the compassionate and loving God and Father of our Lord Jesus Christ ought to break our hearts. I think of a husband who was going through the agony of seeing his wife eaten up with terminal cancer. They both knew that the end of her earthly life was near.

"Have you talked with her about death and shared your feelings with her?" I asked.

"Oh, no, we are believing God!" he said.

Those two things—believing God and facing the fact of impending death—were mutually exclusive in his mind. Why? Is God uncomfortable with facing the reality of death? Is it some gigantic heavenly failure when a Christian dies? How can the death of his saints be "precious in the sight of the Lord" (see Ps. 116:15) and he not let us talk about it? What kind of God keeps people mute and apart at the very time they desperately want and need to be together, sharing their final precious moments? Even pagans are allowed that much!

SOURCES OF OUR CONCEPTS OF GOD

We can avoid the tragedies that flow from a warped understanding of God only by gaining a true view of him.

But how can we find such truth? A rather silly story about some lost car keys illustrates how truth is *not* found.

It seems a man who had been drinking far too long was down on all fours under a lamppost one night looking for his car keys. As people passed by and saw him there, some tried to help, but in vain. At last one of the searchers asked the man, "Are you sure you dropped them here? We've looked and looked."

"Naw," said the man, "I dropped them up the street half a block, but the light is better down here."

People tend to look for God the way this poor fellow looked for his keys. They don't look where they lost him but where the light seems good.

We "lost God" through disobedience and pride and rebellion. We turned away from God in our hearts. We "find God" when in humility and an obedient spirit we turn to God in our hearts. As God told Israel, "You will seek me and find me when you seek me with all your heart" (Jer. 29:13).

The human heart, however, is a dark place, so we have a tendency to look under the lampposts of human teaching, in a manmade system of one sort or another. (Some, of course, come to the conclusion that there probably is no God, at least not a personal God who is interested in them and concerned about their welfare.)

To realize how common the lamppost phenomenon is, you need only answer the question, *What is the source of most people's beliefs about God?* I think you will agree that people generally believe as they do about God because that is what they were taught.

It's easy for us to see that this is true of others. Why are millions of people Muslims or Hindus or Buddhists? Is it not in most cases because they were taught those religions from earliest childhood? Don't the followers of false cults believe their outlandish doctrines because they have been caught up in a system that has brainwashed them?

People also get many of their ideas about God from under another lamppost, their culture. Unless something influences us otherwise, we adopt the values and beliefs of our culture quite unconsciously.

One implicit message of Western culture right now is that there probably is a God, but he is not directly involved with us at any level. God is a personification of good, and there is also evil, but neither God nor the devil are actual persons to whom we relate.

Sometimes the influences that shape us are those of our own subculture rather than the dominant culture. This is true for those caught up in cults. It is also true of the many young people who through mind-altering drugs have tried to get beyond themselves to a new and wonderful "spiritual" experience. Their trips end in disillusionment and often in death or permanent brain damage. No keys to finding God are under these lampposts.

Many people have also clustered under the lamppost of personal "freedom" seeking life's keys. Freedom, uninformed by the presence of God, leads to free love and free sex, free abortions and free homosexuality. Instead of finding God, the searchers find only pain, heartache, disease, torment, fear, and AIDS. Under this lamppost the light has gone out.

So, then, there are all kinds of lampposts under which people seek keys to life and keys to finding God. Some lampposts are more remote from where the keys actually lie than others. What's important to realize is that human indoctrination and culture, even when it is benign, cannot reveal God to us.

Now comes the big question. Are we who happen to be Christians any different in this respect from others? That is, do we believe as we do about God simply because that's how we were taught or influenced by culture? For many people who consider themselves Christians, there may in fact be no difference. The source of their beliefs is human indoctrination.

Jesus said he would build his kingdom on a quite different principle. He did not simply build a better lamppost but specifically said his kingdom would not depend on any human lights. When Peter called Jesus "the Christ, the Son of the living God," Jesus replied, "Blessed are you . . . for *this was not revealed to you by man, but by my Father in heaven*" (Matt. 16:16–17, emphasis added).

This dynamic of *personal revelation* to us from God is the one thing that brings us to know God (as distinguished from simply accepting a system of thought about him). God then guides us in the beliefs we embrace concerning him. We do not simply believe what we are taught, hanging around under the lamppost whether any keys are there or not. Instead, we look directly to God, who turns our darkness into light by his own power. This doesn't mean we can't learn anything about God from other people, but it does mean we test whatever they say by the Word of God and the inner witness of the Holy Spirit.

We must say more about what it means to have God reveal himself to us. How does it all happen? Why does he reveal himself to one person and not another? First, let's consider a couple of other ways people go astray.

MAKING GOD IN OUR OWN IMAGE

We can hardly conceive of a God utterly different from ourselves. It is much easier to create a being patterned after the best in us, blow it up to ultimate dimensions, and crown it "God." But God is not simply a bigger and better one of us.

That's the game the Greeks and Romans were playing long before Jesus came. Their gods and goddesses cavorted through the heavens doing and sanctioning all the things man wanted to do himself. Those gods were simply the deification of human traits and desires.

Conceiving the deity to be like man to the nth power did not go out with the Greeks and Romans. We easily construct a God who thinks the same way we do about morals, behavior, prosperity, healing, divorce, speaking in tongues, the Book of Revelation, honesty, sex, politics, and the American dream. The list goes on ad infinitum. We construct our mythical God, then fight, spit, and scratch to defend him. Anyone who does not align himself with God as we view him is a sinner.

The Bible does teach that man was made in the image of God (see Gen. 1:26–27). It follows that there must be similarities between us and him. How do we accommodate that fact without also creating a mythical, manlike God?

For one thing, we must keep in mind that the revelation we have received is limited and incomplete. Our glimpses of God, even when they are accurate, can be misleading if we take them to be complete. It is true that man was made in the image of God and, therefore, there are likenesses between us and him. The problem is, because of the warpage of sin and because we were separated from God as our life support for so long, we don't really know what that image means. We may identify as Godlike those very traits in us that are least like him. We can end up with a distorted and extremely warped God, and we won't even know at what points the distortions exist.

Recently there came in my mail a vicious racist attack against blacks and Jews. Among other outrageous claims was one that there was biological proof that blacks mated with apes to reproduce Satanic offspring; "This filthy evil is hidden from whites by Jews." At the end of this horrible

diatribe came the following incredible statement: "After
Noah's flood, Satan created Negroes, Asiatics, etc.; Jesus
and God are white men."

Satan is a creator? God is a white man? Both of these
statements show total ignorance of the biblical concepts of
God and of man. This is a radical example of what I mean.
The racist creates god in his own image—a god who is not
only white (and human!) but who hates nonwhites and
considers them the offspring of Satan.

A vicious circle is completed. We have already observed
that people become like the god they worship. At the same
time, people also tend to create God in their own image.
The racist creates a racist god, and in worshiping such a
god he becomes more fanatically racist.

We aren't all virulent racists, of course, so we don't all
distort God's nature along racist lines. Compared to the
pathological and monstrous errors we have cited, our
own erroneous portrait of God may be quite benign. Still
error is error, and it is especially serious when it concerns
God.

Project on your own mental screen the kind of God you
worship. What is he like, and how do you respond to him?
When I first did this, I was shocked to discover how severe
was the God I worshiped. He was rather impatient. In fact,
one thing I've learned since I thought I knew it all is that,
to a large degree, I had imagined God to be a glorified
version of myself. He was endowed with most of my
weaknesses, only in a grander dimension. Is that what God
is like truly? Is he just a bigger one of me?

No, I must not make God in my own image.

Is God Like Your Father?

It is significant to me that Jesus always referred to God as
"father." He used no other term. He came as the Son, and
his purpose was to reveal the Father. He could have come

in any number of other representations: as a prince to reveal the king for instance. But he didn't.

In the 39 books of the Old Testament, God is referred to
as "father" only 8 times—in Psalms, Isaiah, Jeremiah, and
Malachi. In the 27 books of the New Testament, God is
called "father" 242 times. Of those, Jesus was the source no
less than 168 times. That is an amazing thing to me. It
seems God saw that in our alienation we were fatherless
children, and he acted to change that forever. Jesus
promised the disciples, "I will not leave you as orphans"
(John 14:18).

To be an orphan is a wrenching thing. Our youngest
boy, Sundar, came to us as an orphan from India when he
was two years old. At this writing, he is twelve and well
on his way to becoming a wonderful and godly man.

I clearly remember the day Sundar appeared with us
before the judge who was to sign the final adoption papers. It was just over a year from the day we met him as
he arrived in Vancouver, British Columbia.

As our court date approached, we told Sundar what it
would mean. Then, the night before the big event, I explained, "Sundar, tomorrow we will dress in our best
clothes and our whole family will go to see a judge. We
will take a big paper with us. The judge will sign the paper, and that will mean you officially belong to us and no
one can ever take you away. You will never be an orphan
again. You will be our very own son, just like your brother
Jamie."

I can see him now, looking at me with those black, shining eyes. "Will I really belong to you forever?"

"Yes, forever!"

The judge was a friendly, smiling black woman. I've
always thought God especially picked her out for our
brown-skinned boy. She invited Sundar to come and sit on
her lap. With the three-year-old in place, she asked each

member of our family how we liked having Sundar in our home. Then she read the official document we had brought. She asked Sundar if he liked his new family. He assured her we were wonderful.

The judge picked up her pen very deliberately, signed her name, placed the document back in its manila envelope, and handed it to Sundar. What a wonderful day! He now belonged. He had his own family—a real dad and mom and even his own brother and sisters. This little orphan had come to us with a borrowed name, not even sure how old he was, having no one. Now all that had changed forever.

I will never forget how he took that great envelope, put it under his arms, and carried it himself. He would let no one else hold it. He took it to bed with him. He hauled it around with him until it was wrinkled and worn. It was his proof that he belonged to someone. He had a father and was no longer an orphan.

That is what Jesus came to do for us. He came to give us our Father. We are not orphans any more and will never be again. Jesus brought us to the Father. Now we have a name and a purpose. Now we belong.

Yet, when we describe God as our Father, it is a heart-wrenching thing for some people. This world has produced some very poor fathers, and all human fathers are imperfect. Fathers sometimes abandon their children. They beat them, ridicule them, ignore them, have no time for them. Some exploit their children, use them, push them too hard, or control them too rigidly.

I have a wonderful mom and dad. They gave me the gift of growing up in a home where I was loved. I never had to wonder what they thought of me. I never heard the words, "You're no good" or "Why are you so stupid?" I was shocked to find out that some of my young friends were fed a steady diet of such statements. But as wonderful as

my home was, and as loving as my father was and is, God
is not a big one of him. Having a loving father helps me to
understand and believe in a loving heavenly Father, but I
must never make God in any man's image, not even my
father's.

Again we come to the basic principle. I can know God
only as he reveals himself to me. I cannot know him by
embracing a system of teaching about him. I cannot know
him by looking at myself or my father and projecting the
best in us to its ultimate dimension. God must reveal himself, and he does that through his word—through the
written word called the Bible and through the living Word,
his son, Jesus Christ. We still need to explore how it all
happens and we will, in the next chapter.

5

Still More about God

To be quite honest, I have had a lot of trouble with the God of the Old Testament. I believe in him, and I believe the Old Testament, but I don't always understand him. He seems capricious to me and rather severe.

Part of the problem is that in the Old Testament we see God through the eyes of the nation of Israel. Here was a people who had grown up in Egypt as slaves. They were brought out of Egypt by means of devastating plagues visited upon the stubborn Pharaoh and his nation. Their life was full of violence and pain and struggle and warfare. The Old Testament is inspired by God; it also inescapably reflects the culture of the people to whom and through whom it came.

In addition to this cultural influence, the Old Testament also illustrates the fact that God's revelation of himself is progressive. The revelation unfolds more fully as one advances through the Scriptures, and it comes to its fullest light only in Jesus Christ himself.

Some of the early fragmentary glimpses of God can therefore be misleading. God may appear to be bloody and vindictive and remote. As we see more and more of God, even in the Old Testament, a different picture emerges. David is an interesting case in point because

Scripture calls him "a man after God's own heart." David was in many respects a bloody man. He killed many people, and he did it in the name of God. Yet notice what David said late in his life to his son Solomon:

"I had it in my heart to build a house for the Name of the Lord my God. But this word of the Lord came to me, 'You have shed much blood and have fought many wars. You are not to build a house for my Name, because you have shed much blood on the earth in my sight. But you will have a son who will be a man of peace and rest. . . . He is the one who will build a house for my Name'" (1 Chron. 22:7–10).

The true nature of God was not represented by bloodshed but by peace and rest. In fact, bloodshed was so contrary to the nature of God that the man who shed blood, even though it was necessary, could not build the house of God.

Coming as it does from a primitive people steeped in violence, the Old Testament is a remarkable revelation of God as "the Lord, the compassionate and gracious God, slow to anger, abounding in love and faithfulness" (Exod. 34:6).

Yet it remains for the New Testament to reveal God more fully to us by means of the Incarnation. In the New Testament, God not only *speaks* to us in our darkness and confusion but he *comes* to us in human flesh. Although we still inescapably see him through the eyes of our own culture, there is now a new dimension. God has come into humanness! No matter how culture changes, I can understand humanness. God has come in the flesh!

THE GOD REVEALED IN JESUS CHRIST

Left to himself, man is in the dark about the nature of God. Just how dark is suggested by the horrors of human sacrifice and temple prostitution described in *The Source*.

The Old Testament sheds a great deal of light on the nature of God, but we see him indistinctly, through cloud and mist. The New Testament is like coming into bright sunlight by comparison, and the New Testament revelation of God centers in the person of Jesus Christ.

We read, "No one has ever seen God, but God the only Son, who is at the Father's side, has made him known" (John 1:18). The expression "God the only Son, who is at the Father's side" refers to Jesus Christ, as the context makes clear. Jesus Christ makes God known to us. He is the only clear and accurate revelation of God. All other revelations are fragmentary.

God is both like and unlike man, who is made in God's image, but fallen. God is both like and unlike the best of our human fathers. God is both like and unlike the impressions we may get of him from the Old Testament. God, however, is altogether like and not at all unlike Jesus Christ. This is the clear teaching of the New Testament and of Jesus himself.

Consider the following passage from John 14:6–9:

Jesus answered, "I am the way and the truth and the life. No one comes to the Father except through me. If you really knew me, you would know my Father as well. From now on you do know him and have seen him."

Philip said, "Lord, show us the Father and that will be enough for us."

Jesus answered: "Don't you know me, Philip, even after I have been among you such a long time? Anyone who has seen me has seen the Father."

Now here is a truly remarkable thing. Jesus revealed the Father to his disciples, but they missed seeing him! They were still saying, "Show us the Father" even though Jesus had done precisely that. And we are often just like those disciples. We think we see God in all kinds of places where he isn't clearly revealed, but then we miss seeing him in the one place where he is clearly revealed—in Jesus Christ.

Paul put it like this: "For in Christ all the fullness of the Deity lives in bodily form, and you have been given fullness in Christ" (Col. 2:9–10). Or again, "He is the image of the invisible God, the firstborn over all creation" (Col. 1:15).

Those words translated "image" and "firstborn" are interesting. The first is the Greek *eikon,* which means "likeness." Christ is the image or perfect likeness of the Father. The second word is *prototokos,* which is suggestive of our word "prototype." Whenever a new line of cars or planes is to be developed, the manufacturer first produces a prototype—a working model on which the entire new line is based. Christ is the exact likeness of the Father and also the first of a new line of human beings, not to be produced but to be born of the Spirit (hence the use of *prototokos* rather than *prototypos*).

BUT WE CAN'T SEE CHRIST EITHER

To say that Christ is the best and truest revelation of God may not be entirely satisfactory to some. Tell them that no one has ever seen God except as Christ has revealed him, and they might reply, "Yes, but neither we nor anyone else alive today has seen Christ either! What good is a revelation through Christ if we have never seen Christ?"

It's a good question. If Christ is the only clear revelation of God, the issue does become one of seeing Jesus Christ and of perceiving him accurately. God is just like Christ, but what is Christ like?

That, of course, is the subject of the New Testament, and especially of the Gospels. We need to look carefully at the portrait painted there. That is the only way we can get a clear picture of Christ. We cannot exhaustively examine the

New Testament for its portrayal of Jesus Christ in this small book, but we can survey some statements Jesus made specifically about himself.

John's Gospel records several statements of Jesus that begin with the phrase "I am." They not only describe what Christ is like, they also constitute a subtle claim by Jesus that he is to be identified as God. The definitive use of the "I am" phrases is found in John 8:58.

In talking about Abraham, who had died many centuries before, Jesus said, "Before Abraham was born, I am!" Jesus did not say, "I was." Even that would have been an incredible claim. "I am" is stronger because it suggests perpetual, continuing existence. It was even more significant to his Jewish audience. They knew that when Moses was called to deliver Israel from Egyptian bondage, God spoke to him from a burning bush that was not consumed. Moses asked God in what name he should go and the reply came, "This is what you are to say to the Israelites, 'I AM has sent me to you'" (Exod. 3:14). Jesus' use of this name amounted to a claim that he was the God of Abraham and Moses. The Jews understood that at once and reacted angrily. "At this, they picked up stones to stone him" (John 8:59).

Jesus used "I am," standing alone, as a claim to being God. He also used "I am . . ." with a phrase following to describe what he (and therefore God) is like. Jesus said:

"I am the bread of life" (John 6:35).

"I am the light of the world" (John 8:12).

"I am the good shepherd" (John 10:11).

"I am the resurrection and the life" (John 11:25).

"I am the vine; you are the branches" (John 15:5).

Meditating on this self-portrait of Christ, considering each phrase in detail, would surely be a worthwhile study, but here we can look at these "I am" sayings of Jesus only briefly. Each pronouncement relates to a practical hunger or need we all have, a need based on our very nature as God has created us.

"I am the bread of life"—Jesus reveals God as the source of nourishment for our spiritual life; without him, an aspect of our being shrivels and dies.

"I am the light of the world"—Jesus reveals God as the one who enables us to see through the dark nights of our soul. He dispels our confusion and leads us from chaos to order. When every direction looks dark, he lights a pathway for us.

"I am the good shepherd"—Jesus reveals God as the one who will make us to lie down in green pastures. Something will always "shepherd" or influence the direction of every person; we do not have the option of self-sufficiency. Most of the influences that control people's lives also damage and destroy them, but the good shepherd lovingly cares for the sheep.

"I am the resurrection and the life"—Jesus reveals God as the guarantor of our eternity. There is a life beyond this one, but that is of little comfort to us unless we know how to get there and that it will be heaven for us and not hell. In Christ we have that assurance.

"I am the vine"—Jesus reveals God as the source of all life and vitality. He is not a remote source like the distant sun that shines upon and brings life to the soil. He is a source to whom we are vitally and organically connected as branches to the vine, and life flows from him through us.

Of course, each of these "I ams" of Christ could occupy the focus of an entire book by itself, but our purpose in this chapter is to show how God is revealed in Jesus. There he is! He enters our world and our lives directly. He has created us for himself, with appetites and desires that only he can fulfill. He has given us an awareness and inner soundings that cannot be touched through our senses. And now Jesus has transcended culture, whether Israel's or ours, and brought the Father to our orphaned hearts.

MORE THAN HUMAN VISION

To those who want to know what Christ is like, having never seen him, we must point to more than human speculation or even the sublime "I ams" of Scripture. We must point to a spiritual revelation from God himself.

We mentioned the case of Peter earlier. When Peter expressed his ringing conviction about Jesus ("You are the Christ, the Son of the living God"), Jesus said, "Blessed are you . . . for this was not revealed to you by man, but *by my Father in heaven*" (Matt. 16:16–17, emphasis added). Paul also wrote about the need to see Christ with more than human vision. "So from now on we regard no one from a worldly point of view. Though we once regarded Christ in this way, we do so no longer" (2 Cor. 5:16). You see, even if you had been on earth when Christ was here, you might not have seen God in him. Many people didn't. They crucified him as a blasphemer precisely because they didn't accept his claims of deity.

So, then, Christ is the true and adequate revelation of God, but you will never know what Christ is like, even by reading the Scriptures, as important as that is, unless the Father reveals Christ to you by his Spirit.

The revelation of Christ to us, or God's disclosure of himself to us, is tied to several things in Scripture. Three that are consistently mentioned are:

- Seeking God
- Loving obedience to God
- Childlike humility

A Seeking Heart

This matter of seeking God is easily misunderstood and misapplied. For many it conjures up the image of a poor sinner on a spiritual pilgrimage to some shrine. To others the image is that of entering a religious retreat to isolate oneself from the world in order to "seek God." Another image is that of committing oneself to a period of fasting and prayer. I suppose those actions could be helpful, but they are not the focus of Scripture when it urges us to seek God.

What is the biblical focus? Take someone who believes that there really is a God. Let this person form the conviction that the true and living God can be known. Let the sense emerge: *I will know him.* The result is a person who seeks God.

Seeking God is Paul interrupting his writing with the exclamation, "O that I might know him!"

Seeking God is a young man sitting with me describing a new and deep hunger: "I've recently become aware that there really is a God. I want to know him. Can you help me?"

Seeking God is my sons and me looking through our telescope at Jupiter and its beautiful moons and murmuring, "There has to be a God, but what could the Creator of such a wonder be like? I want to know him."

Seeking God is the deep conviction that no matter how much we learn of him we will have only begun to understand him. Each discovery lays the foundation for the next.

Loving Obedience

Like seeking God, obedience can be and often is misunderstood. God deals with us first, last, and always by grace. That means our relationship with him is not based on works or performance. God is not grading us to determine whether our obedience qualifies us to know a little more about him today. He is not training us as we would train a dog. "OK, you obeyed; good boy! Here's another doggie biscuit of revelation about me." There is, however, a connection between our having an obedient heart and the Lord showing himself to us. Jesus said, "Whoever has my commands and obeys them, he is the one who loves me. He who loves me will be loved by my Father, and I too will love him and *show myself to him*" (John 14:21, emphasis added).

Why is it that the person who obeys God because he loves him seems to perceive more about God? That is the question Jesus was asked at the time. "But, Lord, why do you intend to show yourself to us and not to the world?" (v. 22). Jesus replied, "If anyone loves me, he will obey my teaching. My Father will love him, and we will come to him and make our home with him" (v. 23).

We get to know people by spending time with them, and we really get to know people by living with them day in and day out. A couple may be in love and spend as much time together as they can. They may think that they know each other well, but when they live together each learns many things about the other that before were unknown.

Jesus said that he and the Father would move in and make their home with the person who loves and obeys him. As a rule, the "world" neither loves nor obeys Jesus, but it is possible to obey him without loving him. We can try to manipulate God, to put God under obligation to us.

We think, "He has to bless me; I kept the commandments." This may creep into our thinking, and we hardly realize it. Someone said to me recently, "I have gone to church for years and done what Christians are supposed to do. Frankly, I'm more confused now than I have ever been.

Why doesn't God help me?" He assumed God owed him something for doing good and right things.

Loving obedience is not a mechanism for controlling God. Loving obedience is the psalmist saying, "Oh, how I love your law! I meditate on it all day long. . . . I have not departed from your laws, for you yourself have taught me. How sweet are your promises to my taste!" (Ps. 119:97, 102–3).

Loving obedience is George Beverly Shea looking at tempting offers that would compromise his faith and then writing, "I'd rather have Jesus than anything this world affords today."

Loving obedience is the girl with shining eyes who has but one overriding concern about any choice she faces: "Would this please the Lord Jesus?"

Childlike Humility

Jesus said, "You have hidden these things from the wise and learned, and revealed them to little children" (Luke 10:21). He also said, "I tell you the truth, anyone who will not receive the kingdom of God like a little child will never enter it" (Luke 18:17).

The thing about children is that they are obviously dependent. How dependent we are upon God! Not only do we enter his kingdom with the humility of a child, but we can keep learning of him only by maintaining that same spirit. When it comes to God, nobody knows it all, but he delights to reveal himself to those willing to be children in his kingdom.

Part 3

A Few Things I've Learned about Others

6

About Others

Some time ago I met a young man who was saved off the streets of one of our major cities. He had lived there since he was eleven years old when he was introduced into child prostitution by a man who ran a string of boys in the downtown district.

When this young man was seventeen, a street preacher befriended him and ultimately led him to Christ. I asked him what he found to be the hardest part of living on the street. I knew he had been cold and hungry, had slept under bridges, and had endured the many ordeals that homeless people face. I thought he would speak of the loneliness or cold or danger—any number of things came to mind.

He didn't mention any of those things. Instead he said, "The hardest part of living on the street was that nobody ever looked at me; people pretended I didn't exist. When they walked by, they'd always look the other way, and I felt like they wished I was dead, and then I began to wish I was dead, because I really wasn't anybody."

Do you know what the man who led him to Christ did? He simply looked at him and said, "Young man, you look kind of lonely, would you like to talk?" That broke him up. He told me, "Other people, if they looked at all, would quickly glance away. But I was a person to him. I mattered. And because I mattered to him, I could begin to believe that I might matter to God, if one existed."

As I listened to that young man, I thought of the times I had averted my eyes from people who were not particularly comfortable to look at, for whatever reason. True, there may have been humane and proper reasons to avert my eyes sometimes. More often than not, however, it was just what the street boy knew it to be—a refusal to recognize someone as a person.

Those who handle security for celebrities understand this. They advise their clients not to make eye contact with anyone in a public setting. "Look straight ahead and keep walking." In other words, treat people as if they weren't there.

One thing I've learned since I knew it all is this: it is easy to look past people and never really see them. I've also learned that you can look *at* people and still not see them.

I have never lived on the streets like the young man no one would look at. I have never been abandoned and rejected. I have, however, experienced the sense of isolation that comes from being looked at but not seen by those around me.

HEY! I'M A PERSON

It was strange. I was surrounded by people paying attention to me, yet I felt absolutely alone. Doctors and nurses checked my chart. They paid close attention to every detail: my pulse, my blood pressure, my temperature, my medication. What they were doing was obviously important, but somehow I felt like they were leaving *me* out.

Surrounded by beeping machines, electronic monitors, and shiny metal, I had a sense of being another object myself, a challenge to the scientific minds of those who probed and poked and stuck needles in me to see what would happen. Of course, they were doing their jobs, and doing them well. I didn't want to change that. But I needed someone to be *with* me, not just around me. I felt separated, lonely.

In the next bed a man was diagnosing my condition for a visitor. Through my drug-induced haze I heard, "Yeah, he had a heart attack. He's a preacher, you know. Just sitting around all the time, not doing any real work. Finally got to him."

I wanted to defend myself, to explain the high stress of my occupation, to give an account of how physically active I had been—the racquetball games, the running, the biking—but I didn't have the strength. The man didn't see me anyhow, he saw only what "preacher" symbolized to him. So there I lay—an object called "patient" to my caregivers and a symbol called "preacher" to my roommate. No person at all.

I remembered the time I had stood by the bed of my friend, Phil, as a doctor gave him and his wife the verdict: "Two blocked arteries; we'll need to do bypass surgery." I knew nothing of such things then. I had said what I hoped were appropriate words, had offered a prayer, and then left. I meant the words; Phil and his wife were gracious enough to say I had been helpful. But now, looking back, I knew I had not really been *with* them just as most of the people parading through my room were not with me.

A few people were actually with me. Ole, my father-in-law, was one. We hadn't seen each other for several weeks, since before my heart attack and surgery. When he came into my room, he simply said, "Oh, Jerry!" They were words quietly spoken with tears suddenly present. His visit is all I have remembered from the events and visitors of that day. All the rest is a blur, but his quiet voice and sudden emotion are with me as vividly now as then.

There was also my wife, Barbara, quietly reading to me from the Psalms during the late and frightening hours. There was Carmen, our oldest daughter, holding pieces of ice to my fevered lips. And there was Christi, our sixteen-year-old, refusing to leave me even for the short ambulance trip to the hospital; she insisted on riding with me.

There were others too, including some of the people who treated me. They saw me as a person and not simply as a patient.

I remember, during one of the long and difficult nights, a nurse standing beside my bed and softly telling me her story. She described her fear and sense of loss at her father's death a few months earlier. As she told me about her emotions—her doubts, her feelings for her father, her own pain and grief—a strange thing happened to me. Even now, as I write, it seems odd that her story had such a strong, positive effect on me. It certainly didn't seem like the time for her to be talking to me about death.

Why is she telling me this? I thought at first. Then I felt so glad she was. To her, I was a fellow-traveler—one who could understand a little of her suffering because of my own. I was more than a pulse. I was a person, and even in my depleted condition I was somebody to her.

Yet most of the time I was on the receiving end of the kind of treatment I had witnessed from a different vantage point years before. I had once worked in a hospital; it was one of the jobs that helped pay my way through college. I had reacted with shock and revulsion at first when hearing patients referred to as "the cancer in room 201," "the leg in room 209," or "the stomach in 228." Yet the day came when I heard myself, with some chagrin, refer to "the throat in 235." It seemed so much easier to classify diseases and conditions than to see people in pain. And now I had become "the heart surgery in 311."

WAYS WE DEPERSONALIZE OTHERS

It will not do to pretend that those in the medical profession are the only or worst offenders when it comes to treating people as something less than they are. Every day each of us chooses whether or not to treat others as people, and too often we make the wrong choice.

I've already suggested two ways we tend to come short of a full person-to-person encounter with others. We do so by reducing people to objects and symbols. I have explained that in the hospital I felt like an object ("patient") to my caregivers and like a symbol ("preacher") to my roommate. I want now to examine those two attitudes a bit more and to consider a third: reducing people to their functions. Let's look at the third wrong attitude first.

Reducing People to Their Functions

There is no doubt that people serve a utilitarian function in our lives sometimes, much as a machine might. For example, one can throw dirty clothes in an automatic washer or take them to a laundry where a person will receive them dirty and return them clean. One goes to the library to get books and use other library services, not to visit the librarians and spend time with them. However, the fact that I go to the library to get a book does not relieve me from treating the librarian as a person.

Nothing is wrong, then, with using people's services. Nothing is wrong, either, with our need for service being the reason we contact someone. There is something wrong, however, with forgetting that the one doing us a service is a person. We must not see people only or even primarily in terms of their functions. If we see people in terms of function, all that matters is that they perform well. By contrast, if we see people as persons, we become sensitive to their needs and feelings. We care about them.

What do the distinctions I have been making mean specifically? For example, how will I behave differently if I see the librarian as a person rather than as a function? Remember the boy on the street who said that no one ever looked at him? We don't look at people whom we perceive only in terms of their function either. If I am not relating to the person serving me as librarian, I will check out my book and go my way, the quicker the better. My attitude will be, "Don't bother me with small talk and don't bore me with your problems."

But what if I relate to a person? The difference may not seem large, the time it takes is not long, but the effect will be unmistakable. The difference comes from inside me and can best be described as "awareness." I am aware of the person here. I give eye contact. I speak warmly and kindly. My whole manner says, "You are significant; you are something more than a book-checkout device."

Treating People as Symbols

In 1988, soon after American evangelist Jimmy Swaggart came into disrepute for allegedly consorting with a prostitute, Phil Donahue did a television talk show about him. At one point, the studio audience viewed a video of Swaggart's tearful confession before his congregation. While Swaggart wept on film, the Donahue audience hooted and howled in derision at what they judged to be a demonstration of hypocritical theatrics.

I have problems with that. First, the reaction of the audience betrayed their own judgmental attitudes. They had no way to *know* whether Swaggart's show of repentance was hypocritical or sincere, any more than I did. But even worse, they treated Swaggart as a symbol of everything they despised, not as the hurting person that he was. To withhold support of the evangelist, or even to oppose his continuing in ministry, is one thing. To laugh at his pain is quite another.

It's easy to label people as hypocrites or humanists, liberals or conservatives, straight or weird, right-to-lifers or pro-choicers, and on and on. Then we relate to them as symbols of their perceived position, not as people.

Treating People as Objects

Our society has been somewhat sensitized to the problem of treating people as sex objects. Women especially, but sometimes men, feel that they are being used sexually. They feel like prostitutes because they are not valued for their minds or personalities but only for their bodies.

One doesn't have to be a sex object, however, to be an object. One can be a medical object, sometimes called "patient," or a commercial object called "customer," or a production object called "worker," or a control object called "manager." I'm sorry to say also that people sometimes become conversion objects called "souls." This is the case when Christian workers see the unconverted as trophies to be won rather than as people whom God loves and wants to bring into fellowship with himself and his church.

Sometimes our complex "soul-winning" programs contribute to this error. As I wrote earlier in *Love, Acceptance and Forgiveness:*

Christianity is not difficult to communicate. It's simple. We make it hard by our extreme efforts. We give soul-winning courses that take eight weeks or eight months. This communicates to our people how difficult it is to win anyone to Christ.

As a result, Christians are scared to tell anybody about Jesus. They memorize every possible question any non-Christian could ask as well as the correct answers—they want to have all the bases covered. When they have done that we say they are equipped. They aren't equipped, they are incapacitated. We have them so intent on nailing people with the Bible, giving answers to them, that they forget there is a person there—hurting.

Maybe the correct answer does not help. Maybe what a friend or neighbor needs is a cup of coffee to drink and an arm around his shoulder. Someone to listen and care. Someone to exercise the greatest spiritual gift of all—love. It doesn't take a professional to love.

Even within the church, people can become tools to serve a program or cogs in an organizational machine. What a tragedy that is for the church that Jesus intended to carry on his work here on earth!

SOME CALL IT CONTEMPT

Swiss psychiatrist Paul Tournier spent a week at a conference in Geneva with a large number of philosophers as well as scholars from other academic disciplines. The theme of the conference was "The Demand for Equality." At the end of one lecture, Tournier recalls in *The Listening Ear*:

I said to myself . . . that the true problem is contempt. "Don't despise me. Take me seriously." That is what lies behind every claim for equality.

Take me seriously, even if I haven't a university degree, even if I am only a laborer, even if I am black, even if I am an immigrant, even if I am a woman, even if I am an old-age pensioner, even if I am only a little child. The claim is not so much for equality as for dignity, to be taken seriously, to be recognized as a person.

Is it too much to ask to be recognized as a person? Isn't that the minimum respect we deserve and, therefore, also owe to others? I think it is. Yet I remember an outcast, alone on the streets because nobody would look at him. I remember a pastor, alone in his hospital bed because those who looked at him could not see the person there. I see all kinds of situations in which people are treated in terms of their functions or as symbols or objects. And in my heart I know that I, too, have been often around people but not with them. In the next chapter, we'll explore how to make things different, how to treat others as important, as people.

7

More about Others

How can we make sure we give others the respect and recognition they deserve? Simple awareness helps here, but this "simple" awareness is not really very simple. To be alert to the personhood of those around us takes time and attention, often at the very moment when we are absorbed in something else.

For example, I was interrupted while writing this page, and it irritated me. The person calling on the telephone needed to see a pastor. I was invited from my task into the life of a hurting person and found myself annoyed by it. Ironic that I should so illustrate my point!

Too often we get absorbed in our tasks to such a degree that we reduce people to the category of interruptions. So now we have a fourth depersonalizing attitude to go along with the three mentioned in the previous chapter. We treat people as:

1. Functions
2. Symbols
3. Objects
4. Interruptions

It is easy to excuse ourselves for seeing people as inter-ruptions when we are absorbed in a task, as I was today. The fact is, however, that we may always be "absorbed in a task" if we allow ourselves to be. We are always doing something, even when we are resting, and we can always view intrusions into our space as interruptions. Thus, be-ing absorbed in our task may be a form of being self-absorbed.

Awareness of others is a matter of focus. If we lack this awareness, we simply don't see people. It doesn't matter how busy we are or aren't. Even while we're walking or driving between tasks we may still be absorbed with them and oblivious to the people around us. Preoccupation can become habitual.

Two of my professors from seminary illustrate what I'm trying to say. One lived in his own world of ideas and books. I never saw him without something in his hand to read. He shuffled through the halls, oblivious to everyone and everything, his pockets stuffed with papers. The man was a genius. He could recall whole sections of books he had read. The way his mind worked captivated and in-trigued his students, but he remained totally unknown, living somewhere in his own detached world.

The other prof knew nearly every student by name. He was often late for class because he was talking with one student or praying with another. We learned from him, but we were more inspired by him. He always had time for us. Still, I had to admit that his classes would have been better had he spent more time studying and teaching.

We need balance in this. We are not talking about trying to establish a life-long, meaningful relationship with every person we meet. We aren't talking about spending all our time chatting so that we never get our work done. How-ever, we are talking about giving each person we meet the wonderful gift of significance. We are talking about getting out of our self-absorption enough to *see* other people.

AWARE AND ALIVE

In addition to getting out of our self-absorption, awareness also requires what I call "aliveness." Sometimes a certain numbness takes over our lives. Perhaps it's our way of dealing with the constant invasion of sounds, sensations, and activities around us.

I think I saw this numbness most clearly in Manhattan when I was last there. I had the misfortune of being in mid-Manhattan at noon. It was a circus. People were rushing in every direction. Cabs were tearing along, sometimes jumping the curb to get around a car or pedestrian. Horns were honking. People were bumping into one another, hardly acknowledging each other's presence.

A friend and I went to a deli for lunch. We ran for a table we saw vacant. The harried waitress yelled across two other tables, demanding to know our order immediately. I was not quite fast enough and earned a glare from her for being too stupid to know what I wanted.

I noticed people's eyes. No one looked at anyone else. Each person was in his or her own world. Eyes were glazed. Ears were plugged with portable tape players and radios. We were all crammed into one small place, yet we might as well have been on different planets.

Awareness demands that we shake off the numbing effect of our hectic society and be alive to our surroundings. We can see beauty and color where most see only drabness. We can hear music where most hear only a confused clamor. We can feel and sense and reach out to others. Surely this is what our Lord Jesus Christ intends for us. Jesus declared, "I am the life." Those who followed him were quickened, made alive, not only for eternity but in the here and now.

On a recent trip to Switzerland, I met a remarkable eighty-three-year-old Jewish woman. She attended several of my lectures and at the close of one came rushing up to me. In her English, complicated by a German accent, she asked if she could talk with me after the next day's session.

We met on three consecutive days. She was vibrant, alive, and in love with Jehovah and with Jesus, her Messiah. She talked with such enthusiasm, she could hardly contain herself. I was amazed at how many people wanted to stifle her, to quiet her excitement. Not me! I wanted some of her zeal to splash over on me. When I write about "aliveness," she defines it.

I'm not suggesting we can all be bubbling, effervescent fountains of enthusiasm. But we can be alive. We can see and experience the now. We can be aware of the people in our lives. We can live in a world of people rather than a world of things or activities or ideas. We can give the gift of significance to those who touch us.

SEEING PEOPLE WITH THE EYES OF CHRIST

A remarkable thing about the ministry of Jesus is how much of it happened during interruptions. He would be on his way somewhere, and someone would come barging in with a need or a question. For example:

As Jesus started on his way, a man ran up to him and fell on his knees before him. "Good teacher," he asked, "what must I do to inherit eternal life?"

"Why do you call me good?" Jesus answered. "No one is good—except God alone. You know the commandments: 'Do not murder, do not commit adultery, do not steal, do not give false testimony, do not defraud, honor your father and mother.'"

"Teacher," he declared, "all these I have kept since I was a boy."

Jesus looked at him and loved him. "One thing you lack," he said. "Go, sell everything you have and give to the poor, and

you will have treasure in heaven. Then come, follow me"
(Mark 10:17–21).

Notice, Jesus *looked* at him and *loved* him. This young man
kneeling in the dirt in front of him took precedence over
Jesus' travel plans. He looked at the young man and saw
someone to be loved. This account reminds me of another
young man, whose story I recounted earlier, although the
two men are from opposite ends of the social register. People need to be seen and recognized as persons whether
they are "somebodies" or "nobodies" in the eyes of society.

Jesus did not allow the interruption to keep him from
seeing the person. He also did not allow a doctrinal discussion to blind him to the person. Usually when we get
into doctrinal discussions they result either in agreement
(because people accept our views) or conflict (because they
do not). In either case the focus stays on concepts. This
reduces the other person to a supporter or an opponent of
our views. We are back to making symbols of people once
again.

It is so easy to have what we believe is right doctrine
and be proud of it and at the same time not see people.
Jesus devoted a parable to making that specific point. We
call it the story of the Good Samaritan (Luke 10:25–37).
Two religious leaders ignored a wounded man lying along
the road. They didn't see a person there but an inconve-
nience to avoid. In fact, their doctrine prohibited them
from touching a dead body and insulated them from helping this man who had been "left for dead." However, a
Samaritan, whom Jews would despise as a heretic, saw in
that crumpled heap a person worth helping, and he
stopped to care for him.

Jesus told the story and then said, "Go and do likewise"
(v. 37). We are summoned to view people as persons, each
one individual, significant, and important.

GOD'S VIEW OF PEOPLE

People—you and me and all the others on this planet—matter to God. We have intrinsic value and are singularly special to him. Think about it. When man fell, God did not choose to get rid of him and make a new creature. That would probably have been a more efficient way, and certainly a less painful way, for God to handle the whole business. "Chuck this wretch; let's start all over. This loser can incinerate along with the planet." But, no, God chose to let the planet die, which it will, but save the race. And he will give us a new earth on which to live.

That's a profound truth, and it says volumes about the intrinsic value of human beings. God established our value in the very beginning. God did not make human beings in the same way he made everything else. The rest of creation God spoke into existence. He uttered the word and, boom, it was there. Not so with man. God *formed* man out of the dust of the earth. He took a rib from man and *formed* the woman (see Gen. 2:7, 22).

We, then, are a contemplated creation. We were in the mind of God, and he specifically formed us with his hand. That's not true of any other animal, plant, or thing on earth. God didn't personally form cows or monkeys or fish. He spoke, and they were there, the product of instant generation.

Another fact is also important in this regard. God breathed into man the breath of life (see Gen. 2:7). This uniquely formed man is not only biologically alive but also spiritually alive, animated by the very breath of God.

After God had formed Adam and Eve, he commanded them to begin populating the earth. Each new person was to be formed through an act of love and intimacy between the man and the woman. God intended each human being to be the expression not only of his love but also of tender love between a married man and woman. And it is a terrible perversion with tragic consequences when this love is lost, and children are denied their proper parenting and nurture.

If we are to treat others as people, we must keep sight of the divine perspective. In a world that reduces people to functions, objects, symbols, and interruptions, in a world that denies people their birthright of tender love, we can treat them right only as we cultivate the values and attitudes Christ exemplified and taught.

THE RISKS

When we choose to be truly with people rather than just around them, when we treat others as valuable persons, we take certain risks. We could get hurt. Let me suggest four areas of risk and ways we can respond.

1. Rejection

There is a definite possibility, if you extend yourself in some significant or even small way to another person, you may be rejected. Rejection hurts. Naturally, you don't want to set yourself up for painful rejection; you'd have to be emotionally sick to enjoy that prospect.

The question is whether you will allow the fear of rejection to paralyze you. If you reach out to others only when you feel sure that they will respond warmly, if you open up only when it's completely safe, you'll have a lonely existence.

To overcome the fear of rejection, I suggest you remind yourself of three facts:

Fact 1: Rejection is inevitable. Short of retreating from others altogether, there is no way to protect yourself effectively. Actually, we'd be more correct to talk of the fact of rejection rather than the risk of rejection. Even God, when he came to reach out to us in the person of Christ, experienced rejection, and you can be sure you will too.

Fact 2: Rejection won't kill you. You are tougher than you think. You can be rejected and still survive, strong and healthy. That does not mean you will enjoy the experience, but it does mean you can get through it.

Fact 3: Since rejection is inevitable but not lethal, there is no reason to give in to your fears. Why deny yourself the joy of reaching out to others just because some people along the line will reject you? It's a given, part of the price of being human. Accept it and go on.

2. Emotional Involvement

We live in a society where people seldom touch one another's lives. Often our "best friends" are people we are not really close to at all. We have little idea what is going on in each other's innermost lives. Most people, if they have major personal concerns or pain, have no one to talk to except for a professional counselor.

Someone who actually sees us and cares for us as a person can easily capture our hearts. This can lead, and often has led, to improper affections and into illicit affairs. Both in and out of the Christian community, people are reaching out to each other only to find themselves emotionally and then sexually involved.

What a shame that love is so rare that when we think it happens it sweeps us off our feet! We are so impoverished by lack of love and find it so wonderful to receive that we lose our heads.

The response to this risk factor seems to fall between two lines. One is to stay detached and keep our emotions down, but this is precisely the attitude I've been lamenting. It blocks us from treating others warmly and personally. It spiritualizes coldness and rules out compassion.

The other extreme is illustrated by the groups who've encouraged their members to cultivate soul mates. Your soul mate would be a person of the opposite sex (not your spouse) to whom you could reveal your deepest heart and with whom you would "connect." For many people, the partners in these sanctioned connections become sex partners also, and the resultant havoc in their marriages is woeful.

Scripture suggests another way between these two extremes. Paul told Timothy, "Treat . . . older women as mothers, and younger women as sisters, with absolute purity" (1 Tim. 5:1–2). One can have a loving and caring relationship with another person without being sexually involved. We know this is true because many people have such relationships with family members.

But suppose an improper sexual attraction develops between me and a friend. Such a thing is always possible. What then? Then I need to keep straight the proper role of emotions in my life. We Christians too easily buy into the idea that our emotions are commands to act. This works out as follows: "I feel sexually attracted to another person; I must act on that emotional drive or I am in some way being untrue to myself." This is simply false. *My actions need to be controlled by my values not by my emotions.* This principle is extremely important, and I will deal with it more fully in chapter 9.

Of course, it isn't always easy to live by our values, but it can and must be done. In fact, it is being done by the great majority of Christian people the world over. We just don't hear their stories of success and loving service to others. Healthy caring relationships in which men and women behave with Christian maturity and discretion don't make headlines. Virtue has never sold as well as scandal.

3. Getting Hurt

A third risk involved in treating others as people is that we might get hurt. The other two risks—rejection and sexual attraction—also involve pain, but we can get hurt without those two elements.

We can deal with the risk of getting hurt much as we did with rejection. It will happen, but it is not lethal. We will heal and usually will be stronger than before. The joy of loving is worth the risk of getting hurt.

I have some friends who have opened their home to children waiting to be adopted or placed in foster care. These children are with them for only a short while. They could have reason to say, "We try not to get emotionally involved; we don't want to get hurt." They have done the opposite. Their attitude is: this child may be unwanted or abused, but while he is with us we will love him. They know it hurts when a child you love is taken away, but their joy in loving is worth the pain of separation.

4. *Being Misunderstood*

We may act with honest and loving concern and yet be misunderstood. In such a case, we have some recourse. We may be able to explain our actions. Scripture puts it this way, "Do not allow what you consider good to be spoken of as evil" (Rom. 14:16). Good advice! But if you can't win your case, don't let that stop you from loving people. Being misunderstood for doing good is no fun, but it puts you in some fine company—the same thing happened to Jesus.

So what have I learned about others since I knew it all? Something quite basic, really. I can state it in a simple resolution: I will remember that others are valuable human beings made in the image of God and I will treat them not as functions or objects or symbols or interruptions but as persons for whom Christ died.

Being *with* others will have its risks; I have identified some of them. But not being *with* people, being isolated, not only has risks but also certain predictable consequences.

Growing loneliness. Depleted emotional health. Fear and anger that ultimately grow from having people around but never with us. Resentment at believing no one cares about us or understands our longings.

I once met a street person. He had nothing. But he said, "The hardest part was that nobody ever looked at me. I began to wish that I was dead. . . ."

Part 4

A Few Things I've Learned about Ministry

8

About Ministry

Almost ten years ago, Stan Baldwin and I collaborated on a book entitled *Love, Acceptance, and Forgiveness.* What I've learned since then in no way invalidates the basic concepts of that book. I believe now what I said then. However, I ended that book with a comma. "I cannot end it with a period because it is an incomplete statement," I wrote. "I am still learning."

There is much about ministry in that previous book. I hope you will read it or read it again as the case may be. Many thousands of people have found it helpful, and it's now been printed in seven languages.

The following brief excerpt gives you some idea of its basic thrust as regards ministry:

[In the church as a field] ministry becomes a positional identity within the organization. That is, if you are going to minister you must be director of something or minister of something or associate something. You will have a title and a position within the organizational structure. As a result, the individual member is easily misled about the meaning of Christian service and is often reduced to a spectator.

In the church as a force the pastoral leadership is . . . constantly endeavoring to facilitate the ministry of the members. This means the pastor carefully avoids usurping that ministry. He does not do the work for the people but involves them in doing it themselves. . . . Ministry is people filled with the Holy Spirit meeting the needs of other people in Jesus' name.

"Ministry" is a professional-sounding word to most of us. It calls up images of clergymen or other church officials, specialists trained to be spiritual guides for others. I suppose that is not all bad. It is, however, quite myopic. Ministry is much broader than that.

Basically, the word "minister" means to serve. The two words are used interchangeably in Scripture. Jesus said, "the Son of man came not to be ministered unto, but to minister" (Matt. 20:28, KJV). The same verse in the New International Version reads: "the Son of Man did not come to be served, but to serve."

When I talk about ministry, I am not just referring to those with professional degrees, official positions, or religious vocations. I am talking about any and every Christian who *serves,* those people who place themselves at the disposal of another's needs. One inescapably ministers out of one's own life and concepts. Although my definition of ministry is unchanged—to the degree I see myself, God, and others differently than before, or more clearly than before—my ministry is affected.

Your ministry will also be affected crucially by the way you see yourself, God, and others. The following examples will serve not only to illustrate that fact but also to flesh out the definition: ministry is "people filled with the Holy Spirit meeting others' needs in Jesus' name." Note these basic elements in the ministry definition:

- I must have an enabling from the Holy Spirit.
- I must encounter a human need that I can address.
- I must act in Jesus' name.

THE ENABLING OF THE HOLY SPIRIT

Paul wrote, "Our competence comes from God. He has made us competent as ministers of a new covenant—not of the letter but of the Spirit; for the letter kills, but the Spirit gives life" (2 Cor. 3:5–6). Paul here raises the fearful possibility that one's "ministry" may in fact "kill." If one's ministry is a ministry of the letter instead of the Spirit, then that will be its effect.

After one of my recent lectures on God and the kind of freedom he desires to bring to our lives, a young lady walked up to me with tears in her eyes. She said, "As you spoke about God and the kind of person he really is and what he wants for me and my life, I began to see that I have been trying to love a God whom I thought was angry and punishing me. I was also presenting that kind of God to the people I tried to help. Instead of helping them, I'm afraid I heaped loads of guilt into their already difficult circumstances." Her defective view of God militated against any life-giving ministry in the Spirit.

This should not surprise us. Scripture forges a close link between the Spirit and truth. For example, Jesus said, "When he, the Spirit of truth, comes, he will guide you into all truth" (John 16:13). This obviously can't happen when we hold defective and distorted views of ourselves, God, and others. Jesus also said that true worshipers must worship God in Spirit and in truth. Once again he links the Spirit and truth, thus underscoring the fact that they are in fact inseparable.

The issues at stake here are immense. It is not that we will do a little better, have more power, throw more weight if our ministry is of the Spirit. No, but we will minister life instead of death! You see, any time a flawed human being attempts to serve God, there is a risk of doing more harm than good. Peter was trying to serve Jesus when he pulled out his sword and cut off the ear of the high priest's servant, Malchus (see John 18:10). Saul was trying to serve God when he persecuted Christians to the death.

Christian ministry is not anything we do so long as our intentions are good. Some of the meanest people in the world, and the most dangerous, are zealous for what they see as a Christian cause. Sometimes one Christian activist or politician will try to serve God by pushing policies exactly opposite to what another Christian activist espouses. Each considers the other to be misguided and his actions detrimental.

I am writing this book in order to minister, but certainly not everything written in the name of God ministers life. The great British statesman Benjamin Disraeli, himself an author, once said, "Nine-tenths of existing books are nonsense, and the clever books are the refutation of that nonsense." Disraeli no doubt overstated the situation by saying that nine out of ten books are nonsense, but some certainly are nonsense or worse. Yet I'm sure that, like me, almost all writers, and certainly Christian writers, think they are putting out a book that makes sense and also ministers.

GIVING ANSWERS CAN BE A DISSERVICE

My own ministry at present involves a good deal of counseling. From that ministry, let me illustrate what being enabled by the Holy Spirit to serve in truth means:

"Should I leave my husband?" a wife asks.

A promising young man says, "Tell me, should I go to Bible school?"

A husband wants to know, "Should I tell my wife I have become involved in an affair with another woman?"

A pastor asks, "Shall I reveal to my elders that I have
been physically abusing my wife?"

These are not theoretical questions I have dreamed up;
they represent actual situations of people who have come
to me for guidance or direction. In each case I refused to
answer the question. The reason is not that I lack principles or the courage to express them. To the contrary, these
are questions about which I have strong convictions and
some spiritual insight. These questions, however, were also
offers of power over another person's life. In posing their
questions, the individuals were giving away responsibility
for their own decisions and lives, even if they were doing
so unknowingly.

Just yesterday I had a conversation with the wife of a
recovering alcoholic. He had been dry for several months,
but in facing a physical crisis in his life he weakened and
took a drink. She asked me, "If he begins to drink again,
should I leave him? What would you do?"

I had to say to her, "I can't answer that, nor do you want
me to. You don't want to know what I would do. What is
the Holy Spirit saying to you on the subject? Are you able
to hear him? Can I help you handle the tremendous fear
you have of your husband regressing into the bottle?"

You see, people must hear the Spirit of God themselves.
They must come to understand how God speaks in the
day-to-day experiences and the crises of life. As God's
servant, I am not mute or passive in these situations—that
certainly would not be ministry—but neither is it my task
to dispense answers simply because someone asks me a
question.

The wife of an alcoholic must be encouraged to make
her own choices and to take responsibility for them.
Nevertheless, I will not abandon her. I will walk with her
and with her husband through this valley. Her husband

must take responsibility for his choices as well. He has only recently come to Christ. I must serve God's agenda in his life, not my own or his wife's. And what is God's agenda? Both of these people must learn to walk with Christ and to follow his voice as he speaks into their experience. The greatest ministry I can have to these people or to anyone is to help them hear and respond to God's voice in each decision they face.

Eric Fromm's book *Escape from Freedom* discusses the question of why the German people gave power over their lives and nation to Adolph Hitler. He concludes that they surrendered this sense of responsibility to avoid the frightening necessity of being finally responsible for themselves. Over and over in the postwar trials we heard, "I was only following orders," as though because it was someone else's idea and command, the individual was absolved of any guilt.

What Fromm describes is not a problem unique to the German nation. It is a common if not a universal tendency of human beings. One reason legalistic systems attract people wherever they occur, whether in political totalitarianism or religious cults, is that they let the followers escape decision-making responsibility by transferring it to the leaders.

Christians give in to this tendency when they give leaders more power over their lives than they should. As ministers we should remember that we are really servants, and we must never accept all of the power that is offered to us. To rob another of discovering what it means to think Christianly under the leadership of the Holy Spirit, just because telling him what to think is easier and faster, is to violate him as a person.

Once again we are faced with the issue raised in the previous two chapters. How are we to relate to others? I have resolved to treat others not as objects—in this case, puppets or robots to do as I say they should—but as persons.

I have been talking about formal counseling situations, but ministry, you recall, means serving in nonprofessional relationships as well. Ministry may be to a friend, to a younger Christian, to your own children, or to neighbors. Whatever the setting, if your ministry is of the life-giving Spirit, you will maintain a deep sense of respect for others as persons.

It is truly liberating to realize that ministry is not defined as dispensing answers! We sometimes get tied in knots and feel helpless because we are afraid someone might ask us a question that we can't answer. We forget that Scripture identifies love as the greatest spiritual gift. Without love we are nothing even if we have all the answers and can "fathom all mysteries and all knowledge" (1 Cor. 13:2).

HOW WIN/LOSE DISTORTS MINISTRY

One thing I learned about myself, you will recall, is that a win/lose mentality is a cultural box, not a divine mandate. Transfer a win/lose mentality into the ministering situations described in this chapter and what will be the result? I am likely to dictate the correct decision in order to win what I would call a "victory" for God. I can't take a chance that my client might choose wrongly; I might "lose."

"But surely," someone will object, "people do need to make correct decisions. Weighty issues of right and wrong are involved." I agree, the issues are weighty. Furthermore, my motives are pure in that I am sincerely concerned that others not miss God's will. Still I must reject the temptation to manipulate and dominate, to use the tools of guilt and fear, adding a strategically placed "the Lord told me" to maneuver people into taking my advice or agreeing with my view.

Not only is manipulation counter to true ministry in the Spirit, but sooner or later it will usually backfire. In her book *Ashes to Gold*, Patti Roberts tells of the night she and Richard were married:

> Right before we left [on our honeymoon], Oral [Roberts] called us into his study. He closed the door, sat down in one of the armchairs facing the stone fireplace and began to cry.
>
> Richard and I just stared at him, disconcerted. For several minutes no one said anything. . . .
>
> Finally Oral spoke. Addressing Richard, he announced that he had had a dream about him and me the night before. If either of us ever were to leave Oral's ministry or turn our backs on God, we'd be killed in a plane crash. That was his total message except to say he loved us both and that we should have a wonderful honeymoon. . . .
>
> Richard and I were horrified. We couldn't imagine what we had done that had angered God so much that He would start our marriage off with a threat. It never occurred to us that maybe it wasn't God who had spoken, but Oral trying to manipulate us to protect the ministry.

Domination, control, and manipulation are never consistent with ministry. This is true for three reasons: because of who I am as God's servant, because of who God is, and because of who other people are.

1. Who Am I? I am a recipient of God's love and complete acceptance. Since his love is already mine, I am not in some win/lose contest that drives me to dominate others.

2. Who is God? God is one who honors and sustains each person's right of individual responsibility and choice. In Eden's critical hour, when it came down to either controlling man or letting him make a wrong choice, God let him make a wrong choice. You know the story. There was a garden, a tree laden with forbidden fruit, a

terrible consequence if Adam and Eve ate. Yet God left the choice in the hands of the people he made.

3. Who are other people? Other people are individuals whose integrity I must always respect and honor, even if they don't.

SERVING IS NOT THE SAME AS BEING SERVILE

I have written at length about the need to respect the integrity of others and have made it clear that proper respect rules out manipulation, control, and domination. There is, however, an opposite error that we must also avoid. This is to allow others to use us, to become servile in the name of serving. This is just as wrong as dominating others and for much the same reason. It denies the integrity of each person, in this case, our own.

Women are especially susceptible to this trap because they may have grown up with a servile mentality, thinking that the only way they can be good Christians is to defer to everybody. Some men fall easily into the trap too, however. They allow themselves to be manipulated by users who clearly imply, if they don't directly state, that a "real" Christian or a "good" Christian would certainly come up with the money they need to get out of their current jam (or do whatever else it is they want).

My wife Barb describes the danger of confusing service with servility in her book *Ordinary Women —Extraordinary Strength:* "A great difference separates Christian service from servility. A woman who knows who she is in Christ . . . has too much self-respect to be trampled, walked on, or treated with disdain. Her life will not be spent as a pawn in someone else's chess game. She does not fall prey to those who dominate by intimidation, temper tantrums, or anger."

Barb went on to say that Jesus washed the disciples' feet and cooked their breakfast, yet he "didn't feel demeaned in doing the work of a household servant." She then writes:

How does this kind of serving differ from the woman we described earlier as the victim? Why is it not servitude or servility? Here's why: Jesus was not a victim. He *chose*. He was not used, manipulated, coerced, or trapped at any point. . . .

When we choose to use the talents, intelligence, and power God has entrusted to us, we do so not to appease expectations; to get someone off our back; or even worse, to coerce, exploit, and damage others, but to bless them.

This is a more genuine serving than that dutiful drudgery put out by the victim. When we, as free agents—strong, valuable, and empowered by God—cheerfully offer our service to others, it is a true choice. Our service is a gift. No mixed motives. No waiting like the obedient puppy for a pat on the head and a few table scraps.

We love because it is our nature to love. We choose loving service as the best way to live our lives.

Hold Those Calls and Letters

I am aware that what I said earlier about not giving people answers when counseling them may have raised questions in some minds, and I don't want to be misunderstood. I am not calling for a nondirective counseling approach á la the Carl Rogers school of psychology. Although that model may have validity in certain situations, it is not what I am advocating.

At times it is necessary to be quite directive in counseling. Recently a young wife and mother came to me, visibly shaken. She began to pour out the story of the terror she was experiencing. Her husband turned out to be nothing like he had led her to believe prior to their marriage. He was not only extremely violent, but he was deeply involved in drug trafficking. She was afraid for her life.

When she asked, "What should I do?" you can bet I didn't

just nod knowingly and ask her what she thought would be best. She needed and received immediate intervention. My questions were not of a reflective nature. They were: "Do you have a safe place to stay tonight?" "How long will you need such a place?" "What about your children?" I had serious matters—ethical, legal, and practical—to take into account. I did not duck these issues on the grounds of respecting her rights of choice.

I was being offered power into another's life here, of course, and I took it. I said earlier we must not take *all* the power offered us. This young woman was in a vulnerable and dangerous situation. Someone had to act for her as well as with her. As the situation unfolded, her options changed. Her husband was caught and convicted. She had to go through a divorce to protect herself and her children. As her life became less chaotic and more manageable, she began to make decisions more independently. To keep her in a cycle of dependency would have been to violate her rather than serve her.

WALKING A FINE LINE

There is sometimes a fine line between necessary intervention and wrongful domination. A teenage girl was visiting in the home of longtime family friends. The husband in the home, a friend of her father, sexually abused her. As clergymen and professional counselors, we had little choice when we learned of it. In cases of child abuse, the law requires that we report it.

Far more than that initial decision was involved, however. The angry and confused father was caught between the story his daughter told him and his loyalty to and trust in a longtime friend. He was asking, "What should I do? Whom should I believe?"

I don't have time to catalog the immense implications for the offending man and his family, his marriage, his place in the church, his children. In each situation, a canyon gapes on either side of the road. As I near the one side an inner voice warns, "Don't take too much power; this is their call." Near the other, an equally insistent demand comes for a clear yes or no. Or perhaps, "You must, or these will be the consequences."

It's complex and it's involved, but it is the nature of ministry in Jesus' name. And again, it doesn't matter whether we are talking about professional counseling, personal friendships, parent-child relationships, or some other ministry. We will serve people best when everything we do is underlaid by a healthy and true understanding of ourselves, of God, and of others.

9

More about Ministry

My definition of ministry is "people filled with the Holy Spirit meeting others' needs in the name of Jesus." I have described how the Spirit leads us into truth about ourselves, God, and others, thus enabling us to have a life-giving ministry to others. Now we focus on the matter of meeting others' needs. Think back to the examples in the previous chapter. What were the real needs of the people who came to me for counseling?

Some needed a listening ear, a person who would let them think aloud about their options, a person who would bring to their attention factors they might overlook, a person who would help them relate God's resources to their needs. Most of them definitely did not need someone to make their decisions for them, although they may have wanted that. A few did need someone to intervene aggressively, but not perpetually.

To minister, then, we must keep focusing on the question: *What do people need?* But this question must always be distinguished from *What do people want?* Needs and wants may be the same, but they also may be very different. What people want is sometimes decidedly not in their best interest, and it is certainly no service to accommodate them. *What do people need?* must also be carefully distinguished from *What do I need/want?* Giving people what they need is ministry. Using people to get what I need without regard to their welfare is exploitation.

NEEDS WE CANNOT MEET

Sometimes we feel frustrated and perhaps guilty because we are unable to minister. People have great, crying needs, and we are powerless to help them.

Not too long ago I was preparing to leave an airplane after a long and crowded flight. Directly ahead of me was a woman laden with suitcases, paper sacks, and shopping bags. She was trying to handle all this baggage and at the same time guide a small child toward the front of the plane.

Not only did she obviously need help herself, but she was also holding up the deplaning of the weary travelers behind her. Several of us offered to help her carry something, but she would have none of it. She glared at us as though we were the meanest most untrustworthy bunch she had ever seen.

With every offer of help, her resolve was only strengthened. She was going to do this her way and by herself! All we could do was watch her struggle toward the door. She finally made it, much more frazzled and frustrated than she ever needed to be.

Sometimes we cannot help others, no matter how much they may be hurting or in need. They need to be willing to trust us enough to allow us to enter into their situations. It is also a fact that we cannot meet every need we see, even when the door is open. We are surrounded by human need and suffering, but every need cannot become our personal assignment. That would be a direct route to exhaustion if not to insanity.

There are, however, many needs we can meet. There are pains we can alleviate. There are people to whom we can bring hope or comfort or encouragement or opportunity or correction.

SERVING THOSE UNWILLING TO BE SERVED

Sometimes God may lead us and enable us to serve the needs of those unwilling to accept our help.

In the Portland area recently, Mettie Williams had a ministry to a man she had never seen before and who wanted nothing to do with her. The man rear-ended the Williams' family Volkswagen as it was being driven by Mettie's son. The man had a blood alcohol level nearly double the legal limit for driving. A police officer had seen the man driving erratically and was just about to pull him over when he rammed the Volkswagen.

Mettie did some investigating and discovered that the man was a regular at a couple of the local bars. She also knew a good deal about the way such offenders were handled. Because he had a clean driving record, he would get off with a slap of his wrist, and no effective action would be taken. In all probability he would go on driving and drinking. Mettie felt in her heart that here was a tragedy waiting to happen. He could kill somebody or maim them and bring ruin not only to other innocent people but to his own family as well.

Mettie wrote a letter to the judge urging decisive intervention. She contacted the prosecutor and volunteered to tell what she knew in court. When the arraignment date arrived, she entered the courtroom and sat down. The defendant was there with his family, including a grown son who looked pretty big and intimidating to Mettie.

The son walked over and said to her, "Are you Mettie W. Williams?"

Mettie said, "Yes, I am."

The man said, "You're the one who's written the judge?"

Mettie said, "Yes, I am."

The man asked, "You're going to ask the judge to show leniency to my father?"

It sounded more like a statement than a question, and Mettie wasn't sure what would happen next. She looked the man in the eye and said, "No, I am not going to ask for leniency. I want your father to get help."

"Thank you," the man said. "We've been so worried about Dad's drinking we've just not known what to do. Maybe now he'll get the help he needs."

Instead of the judge ordering the routine diversion program for the man, he was ordered to a hearing. He ended up getting the kind of intervention Mettie had reason to believe would really make a difference. What a beautiful ministry Mettie performed!

"To minister" means to be available when help is needed, as Mettie was. It means to be open for business in the spirit of Jesus, who came not to be served but to serve. When an obvious need presents itself to us, we must be willing to be interrupted in order to meet it.

Someone gave me a little brass sign to hang on my door. On one side it says, "Out to lunch." On the other side it says, "Gone fishin'." Either way, the message is, "I'm not open for business." That is just the opposite of what I am talking about when I say be available for ministry.

What particular ministry do you need to be available for today or this week? Maybe it's to take that eager youngster of yours to his or her soccer game. Maybe it's to write a letter to an elderly mother or dad who has waited too long to hear from you. Maybe it's to help a coworker whose life is a mess and who needs a little relief from all life's demands.

SERVING IN JESUS' NAME

Christian ministry is people filled with the Spirit meeting the needs of others in Jesus' name. That last part—in Jesus'

name—doesn't mean we always mention Jesus whenever
we do anything for others. Nor does it mean we claim to
have Jesus' authority for everything we say and do. "In
Jesus' name" means we are acting on his behalf and because of him.

To minister in Jesus' name is to acknowledge that apart
from him I would be a taker, not a giver. To minister in
Jesus' name is to assign all the glory and credit to him, not
in an attempt to sound humble and spiritual, but because
he deserves it.

It's remarkable how easily we can distort the phrase "in
Jesus' name" so that it actually becomes an expression of
pride. Stan used to be an editor for a Christian publisher.
Sometimes people would send in manuscripts accompa-
nied by notes disclaiming credit for what they had written. "I got this all from the Lord; it is entirely his work,"
they would say. Obviously, they thought they were being
humble. But in actuality they were making the loftiest
imaginable claim—that they were a direct channel from
God. Stan says the material from such people was invari-
ably of poor quality. "If they really got their stuff from
God, you'd think he would at least know something fresh
to say, not to mention knowing how to spell," Stan
observed.

Another distortion of the concept "in Jesus' name" appears when one preaches or teaches in a way that claims
divine sanction for one's own ideas. A speaker declares
emphatically, "This is not my opinion; it is God's word!"
Well, if all he has done is read Scripture, it would be correct to say it is God's word. Preaching and teaching, however, involve interpretation and application of God's word.
As soon as we begin giving our interpretation or making
application of the Scriptures, the human factor enters.

A pastor came to talk with me after I had addressed a
conference some time ago. He took exception to the way

I had treated a particular section of Scripture. I tried to show him that my interpretation fit the context and the original language of Scripture. After we had discussed the passage briefly, he said, "Well, I don't know about all this Greek and context stuff. I just preach the Word the way the Holy Spirit wrote it."

It would be quite wonderful if we really were so objective and inspired—if we always interpreted Scripture in exactly the right way—but the fact is we are not and do not. What we all preach and teach is *our* understanding of the Word. If our understanding is aided by intelligent study and thought, it is more likely to correspond with God's truth. To deny this is to argue that whatever idea occurs to us while we're reading Scripture is *the* message of God to be proclaimed with authority "in Jesus' name."

I don't mean to imply that, in the case cited above, the fact that I had better studied the passage guaranteed that I was right in my interpretation and that the other pastor was wrong. No matter how much we study, others every bit as spiritual and as knowledgeable as we are may see it and teach it differently. That is simply a fact. So we always need to go easy on declaring our message to be the truth of God "in Jesus' name." When we haven't demonstrated enough humility or diligence to study the passage, claiming divine authority for what we say is all the more misguided.

We must have some humility. When it comes to theology and interpreting the finer points of Scripture, we are all a little off. Of course, we are able to understand God's redemptive plan fully through his inspired Scripture. There's no question about that, but it is also a fact that we read Scripture through the grid of our own background and total life experience. That is why we must never become arrogant and isolated from our Christian brothers and sisters, neither from those in the Body of Christ today nor from those in the Church through the ages.

Our Christian faith is always a matter of both learning and unlearning, of gaining new insights while filtering out wrong or distorted ideas about God, ourselves, and others. This should in no way cause cynicism or shake our faith. The Christian faith is dynamic. It does not flow from static formal creeds, although creeds may have a place. Our faith must grow out of a relationship with God and others. It is refined as we walk with God through the vicissitudes and the victories of life.

MINISTRY AND PRIDE

Few things are more destructive of true ministry for Christ than arrogance and pride in its many forms. Pride of interpretation—being sure that I am the authority on what God's word says and what God's will is—constitutes one of the many forms of pride. Arrogance, pride, and rigidity also rear their heads in other places to distort and inflate our view of ourselves and hinder us from ministering in Jesus' name.

Sometimes we get proud simply because God has used us. No one who has experienced the joy of significantly helping another during a time of crisis or pain easily forgets the exhilaration of it. To be sought out by those in need is one of the greatest honors we can receive. However, the gratitude shown to us and the joy we experience can give birth to a subtle pride that makes us think we really are quite wonderful, certainly important, and even indispensable to others and the kingdom of God.

BURSTING OUR BUBBLES

There is joy in serving Jesus, but there is also a certain joy in serving that Jesus disallows. Jesus once sent out seventy-two disciples to minister. We read, "The seventy-two returned with joy and said, 'Lord, even the demons submit to us in your name'" (Luke 10:17). They were really excited about what they had been able to do. If we had been Jesus, we'd probably have encouraged their reaction, thinking, *Great, they will never forget the thrill of this experience; they will want to serve me from now on!* Instead, Jesus said, "Do not rejoice that the spirits submit to you, but rejoice that your names are written in heaven" (v. 20). Don't rejoice in the power you've displayed but in the grace you've received.

Our joy that someone has been set free from Satan's hold can easily give way to a selfish joy that feeds on our *perceived* significance in being used for such a miracle. This pleasure in one's personal importance nourishes pride while camouflaging the whole scene with spiritual phrases ("Praise the Lord"/"It was really the Lord").

Isn't it interesting in this regard how often Jesus told people he had just healed, and in one case raised from the dead, "Don't tell anyone"? I'm not suggesting we should never describe the miraculous. That was not the practice of the New Testament church, and it should not be ours. I do question, however, parading the miraculous or the miracle worker as is often done today. The church is primarily a guerrilla organization, a leaven in the dough of society. It has never done well from the front pages of newspapers or on the six o'clock news.

Recently a well-known healing ministry came to our city, and a local television station decided to do a special on them. What boosts television ratings is not so much healing as the controversy always surrounding any form of the miraculous in the public media. The net effect of this programming and the sensational teasers that advertised it to viewers was a misunderstanding of what was happening, an overemphasis on the personalities involved, and a boost to the already cynical attitude prevailing in the public toward the church.

As I watched, I knew people were being healed. I also knew some were not. I couldn't help but think this might have been an occasion when Jesus would say, "Go, but don't tell anyone what has happened to you."

When ministry is truly in Jesus' name, we are far more impressed with Jesus than we are with the minister, be that minister ourselves or someone else. Since we are not all that much impressed with what we have done for Jesus, we see little need for declaiming, "The Lord did it; I was just a vessel."

We can be thankful that, unless we take ourselves too seriously, God has little ways of humbling us from time to time. Dale Galloway, pastor of New Hope Community Church in Portland, Oregon, was impressed that he had been asked to speak at an international church growth conference. The conference was held at a prominent hotel. While Dale was going up in the elevator to his room he discovered he had practically no money with which to tip the bellhop.

"You know," he told the bellhop, "I'm an author, and I am speaking at the conference here. I'm embarrassed to tell you that I only have nine cents on me, and I wouldn't want to give you such an insulting tip. But I do have one of my books here. Perhaps you or your wife would enjoy reading it; I'd be happy to give you this copy."

The bellhop thought for a few seconds and responded, "I'll take the nine cents."

Dale thanked the Lord for reminding him that he wasn't such great stuff and laughingly told the story on himself.

A SENSE OF AWE

Pride infects us at a deeper level, however, than just leading us to be impressed with ourselves and our views. The pride I'm talking about now is not so much an inflated view of ourselves as it is a deficient view of God.

When we lose the awe of God, we are most in danger of arrogance rushing in to fill the vacuum. We cease to be learners and therefore cannot be teachers either. We begin to substitute conclusions for discoveries. By contrast, a thoroughgoing awe of God not only enriches our own lives but also becomes the base from which we are able to enrich others.

What I am calling "awe" is much the same thing the Old Testament calls "fear" of the Lord. The Hebrew has other words for dread and for fright or terror. The word usually translated "fear" means reverence, which Webster's says is "profound, adoring, awed respect." This "fear" or awe of God has a powerful effect on our lives, as the Book of Proverbs makes clear:

"The fear of the Lord is the beginning of knowledge" (1:7).
"The fear of the Lord is the beginning of wisdom and knowledge of the Holy One is understanding" (9:10).
"The fear of the Lord adds length to life" (10:27).
"The fear of the Lord is a fountain of life, turning a man from the snares of death" (14:27).
"The fear of the Lord teaches a man wisdom, and humility comes before honor" (15:33).

Knowledge and wisdom and understanding and *life* flow from "fear," from standing in awe before Almighty God. These elements are essential qualities in any person who would step into the lives of people in crisis, pain, or need.

Do you want to know what it means to minister "in Jesus' name"? It means to minister while standing in the awe of God. It means to imbibe something of the spirit of Isaiah, who wrote, "For this is what the high and lofty One says—he who lives forever, whose name is holy: 'I live in a high and holy place, but also with him who is contrite and lowly in spirit, to revive the spirit of the lowly and to revive the heart of the contrite'" (Isa. 57:15).

Sometimes we try to minister when we have little awe of the high and holy God, little awe that such a God should love us lavishly, little sense of a contrite and lowly spirit. So we minister our conclusions, we give our answers, and the people don't know God better but are more dependent on us.

Instead of communicating the awesome love of Christ to people, we feed them straw. We tell them how the Christian life should be lived and load them with guilt for not living it as we say. When they "repent" and knuckle under to our instruction, we commend ourselves for our powerful ministry and become more arrogant than before.

There is a better way, a ministry not of the letter—which kills—but of the Spirit—which gives life. Out of a sense of awe and humility, we can act with power and love in the lives of those around us. Rather than "helping" in ways that cause people to become more dependent on us, we can help them discover the strength and presence of God in their own lives. It's glorious!

Part 5

A Few Things I've Learned about Success

10

About Success

We hear a lot about success these days and how to achieve it. Some of us are pretty sick of the whole subject and more than a little suspicious of those who offer to point the way. These reactions are understandable, given the range of pseudo-Christian and superficial solutions being offered. However, I have noticed that wherever I travel, no matter what the country or culture, people are eager to talk about or show me their accomplishments. People's sense of value and certainly their self-esteem seem universally tied to the "satisfactory accomplishment of something attempted," which is a dictionary definition of "success."

Not only do we want to be successful and recognized as such, but we also attach more credibility to others when we perceive them to be successful. This fact is the given that lies behind a phenomenon known to traveling speakers everywhere, the Introduction. I remember how important introductions were to me when I first started traveling and speaking. Some introductions helped me get started well and others almost paralyzed me.

Once I was introduced for a week-long lectureship by a man who read a lengthy compendium of inaccurate information obviously prepared by someone else and handed to him. I was embarrassed to stand up afterward. I spent the first several minutes correcting misinformation and trying to give a somewhat more realistic representation of myself.

Unbeknown to me, the man who introduced me had stepped out and didn't hear my corrections. To my shock and to the delight of the audience, he stood and read the same introduction the next day. He never did understand why everyone was laughing and clapping as I went to the podium.

An introduction of a speaker assumes that people need to know why they should pay attention and receive what the speaker has to say. Basically, we want to know that the person speaking to us has been a success at something.

Success, then, is a legitimate subject of inquiry and teaching. The problem in our success-soaked society is not that we desire success but rather that we don't know what it is. We have drummed certain aspects of success into the ground and almost totally ignored others. As a result we have some successes all right, often dearly bought, but our lives are characterized by continuing day-to-day frustration and mediocrity.

What is success? I believe I've learned three things about success that I little understood when I was first tagged with the label "successful." Success, I now know, lies in:

1. sharing all of my life with God
2. acquiring God's values for myself, and
3. living by faith.

SUCCESS IS SHARING ALL OF MY LIFE WITH GOD

When our family moved to Seattle, we moved to traffic jams. It's like an initiation rite. You don't really belong until you've been stuffed into one of the floating bridges across Lake Washington at 7:30 A.M. or 5:30 P.M. That is when the official stuffing ceremonies are held, Monday through Friday. Special unscheduled stuffing ceremonies are held at other times, but they are not part of the true initiation rites.

It's an incredible sight! Cars snarl at each other and strain forward like huge iron horses chomping at the bit, as if a show of power would send the others fleeing in fright from the bridge.

At one time I would have been caught up in the useless game, straining by sheer nervous energy to clear the jammed bridge. Now, however, an invitation comes, gently but very clearly. My attention shifts from the snarl, the horns blowing, the anger, the impatience. I begin to see something else.

This bridge floats on a uniquely beautiful lake, nestled like a precious stone in the middle of the metro area. It presents a different sight every day. Its expressions are constantly changing, sometimes even as I watch. The lake seems quite at home and unimpressed by the great buildings and concrete highways of the city dwellers. As I lift my eyes a little, I see the great Olympic Mountains. On clear days they seem to bend closer to be seen in their majesty by those who would respond to the invitation.

The invitation is not simply to admire the creation but to be with the Creator. I don't have to get all stressed out and frustrated because my effort to hurry somewhere has been thwarted. Instead, I can spend these moments embracing and being embraced by the One who created all things. This Creator loves me; he died for me and rose again that I might never be separated from him.

Scripture says, "Neither death nor life, neither angels nor demons, neither the present nor the future, nor any powers, neither height nor depth, nor anything else in all creation, will be able to separate us from the love of God that is in Christ Jesus our Lord" (Rom. 8:38–39). If nothing can separate us from God's love, then traffic jams certainly cannot. However, they can separate us from any awareness of him or his love. Success in crossing Lake Washington, then, is not simply a matter of getting to my destination in good time but also of having a good time in getting to my destination.

In many aspects of my life I've often been so obsessed with arriving that I've missed the journey. I have behaved as if being on the way is a total waste. On-the-way minutes or hours delayed my arrivals, so I resented them.

To change the image slightly, when one is scheduled to speak, it is easy to miss everything else on the program while waiting one's turn to be introduced. Yet most of life consists of waiting to be introduced, of ordinary hours and days that fill our lives between the high moments. Success must encompass those ordinary days and hours, not just the high moments. Otherwise our lives are unsuccessful most of the time.

Dr. Jennifer James, a Seattle anthropologist, addresses this concept in her book *Success Is the Quality of Your Journey*. She writes about the problem involved in basing our success on outdoing others: "We're used to establishing our personal scores by comparison. . . . But there is always someone wealthier, more attractive or gaining in popularity. The prize is always just out of reach."

I think most of us have experienced the frustration of going for this kind of elusive prize. What should we do differently? Dr. James advises: "Put more time into things with no discernible score. Nurture friendships with people outside your competitive sphere. Walk in the woods, read novels, listen to music, meditate, laugh loudly, play with children and animals, secretly pick up litter, give things away."

I think that is all splendid advice. Doing as she recommends will help us to "stop and smell the roses." But we must go beyond all this. That's why I was disappointed with the conclusion Dr. James reached after giving her good advice. She wrote, "You'll win in the long run, if you still want to, because you'll be the prize."

Making yourself the prize and leaving out God won't do. There is a severe limit to the success one can have through realizing human potential. No matter how we package it or sincerely pursue the idea, man just does not do well being his own god. We must worship the Creator and not the creature if our journey is to have quality. Otherwise we are like the hunter whose gun accidentally discharged. The bullet narrowly missed his hunting companion and best friend. The hunter went weak all over, then felt profound gratitude that he had not killed his friend. The trouble at that point was that he had no one to thank. He was not a Christian and wasn't sharing his life with God. The experience led directly to his conversion because he knew he could not say a genuine thank you without someone to say it to.

The humanist approach to life cannot add transcendent quality to the journey. Sharing life with God as he is revealed in Jesus Christ can and does. God's presence in the everyday is the only thing that can deliver us from the mundane and make life a success. God's presence transforms both the stressful traffic jam and the joyfully averted accident into something more, something glorious.

God's presence also transforms the workplace and every other tedious element of life. In his book *Take This Job and Love It*, my coauthor, Stan Baldwin, describes the four conditions that leading authorities say do most to cause harmful job stress:

1. censure or lack of recognition
2. frustration, feeling useless

115

    3. resentment, hatred, and ingratitude
    4. disrespect for your own work

In each case, Stan shows how working to the glory of God alleviates the stressful situation:

1. God himself recognizes and praises our work.
2. By working with a spirit of service we feel useful.
3. We praise and thank God for our job.
4. We reflect God's excellence in our work.

Similarly, we read in 1 Thess. 1:3 about "work produced by faith." This word "work" refers to common tasks, the usual duties of life. As someone put it, "The trouble with life is that it's so daily." But living with an awareness of the presence of God gives even the most common event or task the aura of the eternal, the potential of the miraculous. This is what gives our journey an unfolding and glorious quality. This is part of what true success means.

11

More about Success

Success is not only reaching my destination, it is enjoying the journey. The quality, the potential for joy, of the journey is most enhanced by sharing all of life with God. That's what I've been saying.

SUCCESS IS ACQUIRING GOD'S VALUES AS MY OWN

I have come to understand also that success is found in acquiring *God's values* as my own. The Bible doesn't have much to say specifically about achieving success as our society sees it. I think that is a significant omission. In our society, success means climbing the ladder, winning the game of life, achieving a noteworthy goal. It always involves gaining personal recognition. We want to be able to say, "I've done it; I've beat the odds." Usually we want to add, "Do as I suggest, and you can be successful too."

The biblical perspective is quite different. As we said earlier, life is not a game to be won or lost, although we may think so since we are raised in that box from earliest childhood. Life is not a win/lose game but a gift to be received from a loving heavenly Father. The prize God wants us to seek is not material abundance, either for its own sake or as a witness to our abilities. (Nor is the prize

117

"me," as some propose.) The prize is, in the words of Paul, "the high calling of God in Christ Jesus" (Phil. 3:14, KJV). God has a high calling for me. Whatever I may accomplish and whatever status I may gain, it will mean little if I miss my high calling.

Be clear about this. I am not saying that material abundance and the applause of men and the achievement of goals is wrong. I'm not saying they are ignoble, unworthy, or undesirable. What I am saying is that they cannot make us truly successful.

We are free to set goals, even material and financial goals. We are free to work hard to accomplish things that are worthwhile. We are free to accept and enjoy commendation for work well done. None of that is wrong. But we must understand and never forget that we can have all these things and still not be a success. These things do not add quality to the journey, and even less do they help us win the prize of God's high calling in Christ.

When we read the context of Paul's remark about pressing toward the mark for the prize of the high calling of God, we find it focuses on *knowing* Christ and *becoming* like him (see Phil. 3:8–14). Becoming like Christ requires that his values also be our values.

WHO JESUS SEES AS SUCCESSFUL

Jesus once uttered eight brief statements describing people he called "blessed." I think it's safe to say that to be called "blessed" by Jesus *is* success. In each statement Jesus said that people who act in certain ways or maintain specific attitudes are blessed. Please note that these "beatitudes" are not abstract ideas or principles, as we are inclined to think, but they are descriptions of people.

1. *"Blessed are the poor in spirit, for theirs is the kingdom of heaven"* (Matt. 5:3). The phrase translated "poor in spirit" has negative connotations. "Poor" was generally

used to refer to beggars and those looked down on because of their lack of material goods. Jesus captures that idea here, but his emphasis is not on being poor but poor *in spirit*. Jesus is not teaching that begging is noble or that poverty is more spiritual than prosperity. Rather, he is describing a person who has acquired Christ's values sufficiently to reject material gain as the basis for life.

Material things always regress to commonness. Whether it's a bicycle or a Maserati, a cottage or a mansion, a canoe or a yacht, its wonder soon pales. Isn't it shocking how quickly the luster fades? Jesus said it best, "A man's life does not consist in the abundance of his possessions" (Luke 12:15). Things simply cannot produce a successful life; they can only decorate it.

Centering one's life on money cannot provide real success and in fact prevents it. Whether one gains wealth or doesn't, the money-centered life is a failure because it exalts empty values.

Recently some highly visible church leaders have been exposed for having spent millions of dollars on lavish living. The great public revulsion at these revelations underlines how distasteful and at variance with true Christian values this is. Opulence, greed, and materialism, however, are not new in the church. We have seen it in various forms since Paul warned young Timothy about "men of corrupt mind, who have been robbed of the truth and who think that godliness is a means to financial gain" (1 Tim. 6:5).

Jesus himself waded into the money changers and merchandisers at the temple. He said, "'My house will be called a house of prayer,' but you are making it a 'den of robbers'" (Matt. 21:13).

Throughout history religious leaders have taken advantage of the poor and helpless in the name of God. Those who sold doves in the temple yard in Jesus' time were of the same stripe as those who sold indulgences and built great cathedrals on the backs of the poor in the Middle Ages. Their present-day counterparts prey on widows in order to "build a great ministry for God." They promise, "If you will send $50 to this 'faith ministry,' God will give you back a hundredfold."

The person who is most adept at fleecing people, building a great "ministry" and living like a king, is often proclaimed a success . . . until he falls. Then he is reviled. He was never a success in Jesus' eyes because he was not poor in spirit.

As for his fleeting status, the only status that really counts is not something conferred upon us by a fickle crowd, to be snatched away whenever the tide of opinion turns against us. Real status is hearing Christ say, "I have called you friend, for everything that I learned from my Father I have made known to you" (see John 15:15). Oh, to be Jesus' friend and to have him tell us all he has learned from the Father! That is success.

2. *"Blessed are those who mourn, for they will be comforted"* (v. 4). To mourn means to be touched deeply with grief. Part of our high calling is to be numbered among those who are sensitive to the pain and suffering around us.

I mentioned earlier that I once worked with sick people; I was an orderly in a county hospital. My floor was primarily for terminal cancer patients, people who would never leave those dreary, pain-filled corridors. I was only eighteen years old and had not seen much suffering, let alone death. The first three weeks were like a living hell for me. The cries of the suffering and the faces of the dying formed the stuff of wild and ghastly nightmares when I could sleep.

One evening I was working with a nurse who had spent years caring for the terminally ill. I asked her, "Do you ever get used to this suffering?"

She said something that I have carried with me to this

day. "When you get used to it, do us all a favor and get yourself another job."

The horror and emotional upheaval in fact did go away as I made an important discovery. The more I became acquainted with my patients and took an interest in them, the less emotional trauma I experienced. You'd think it would work just the opposite, and for some it may. But that nurse had given me sage advice. Don't let your exposure to pain steel you against being able to mourn for or feel the pain of others.

One of those I have taken with me in memory from that cancer ward is a man we called Captain Bill. When I met him, he was a stump, having had both legs amputated at the hips and both arms at the shoulders. It had never occurred to me that anyone could live in that condition.

Captain Bill easily read the horror in my mind the first time we met. "Pretty ugly, huh, kid?" he bellowed at me. The amputations had not inhibited either his volume or his language.

Over the weeks we became better acquainted and an unlikely friendship began to grow between the crusty old captain and the inexperienced kid. Gradually his story came out. For many years he had captained tug boats up and down the West Coast and in Puget Sound. Because of his rough life and his drinking, his family had long since written him off. That explained why he never had visitors, nor to my knowledge did anyone ever inquire about him. On my floor, that wasn't unusual.

Captain Bill's call light used to come on late, when everything was quiet, and I knew he wanted to talk. As I write this, that almost-forgotten world comes back to me—the painful nights, the angry nights, the lonely nights. And I remember the night Bill said, "So you're going to be a preacher . . . . So, what do you think? Any hope for a blaspheming old sailor like me?"

Over time, his light began coming on earlier, and we talked longer. We prayed together and read from John's Gospel. There was indeed hope for a blaspheming old sailor.

I remember the night Bill's light came on, and something inside me said, "This is it; he's going to die tonight." I went into his room. Already his wide face was bathed in that strange and telltale moisture that often accompanies the last few hours or minutes. But his eyes were bright. He said quietly, "This is it, preacher. I want you to be with me." He motioned me closer with his chin since he had no arms. "Thank you, son. Let's pray and read a little until God gets here."

I cried then, and I'm crying now as I recall Captain Bill, who came into my life forever more than thirty years ago. Through him Jesus taught me one of my earliest lessons about kingdom values. He was teaching me to mourn. He still is.

It was said of Jesus that he was touched with the feeling of our infirmities (see Heb. 4:15). We are told that we should "mourn with those who mourn" (Rom. 12:15). It's easy to imagine that success ought to be a life untouched by grief, pain, or sorrow. Given the world as it is, however, to live without mourning means becoming a shell of a person, not someone Christ calls blessed or successful.

3. *"Blessed are the meek, for they will inherit the earth"* (v. 5). "Meek" comes from a word that means "power under control." This is far different from weakness, as some understand meekness to mean. In fact, power under control is just about the greatest kind of power there is and the only kind that can be trusted.

Power out of control is responsible for much of the grief in the world today. Political power out of control infringes on human rights. Parental power out of control abuses children. Personal power out of control runs over other people. Physical power out of control produces a bully on the playground or a thug in the streets.

Anyone with power who lacks the inner strength (meekness) to control that power becomes a threat to others. The Hitlers and Khomeinis of this world have power but not meekness. They also have "success" of a kind, but they leave a trail of corpses. Such a person is surely not successful in God's eyes.

Ron Rearick is one of the best examples I know of power out of control that became power under control, or meekness. When I think of his story, which I learned about through his book, *Iceman,* I can hardly believe that the violent criminal described there is the same man I have come to know and love over the past several years.

Ron Rearick was a Mafia strong man. His last crime was to hijack a plane for a million dollars. Ron miraculously met Christ in prison and nearly as miraculously was released soon after by the same judge who had sentenced him to twenty-five years just a few months before.

Although Ron had been converted, he didn't know much about meekness at first. That's clear from his account of an early attempt to witness:

One Saturday, I decided to go to the park and watch how the Jesus People witnessed. These kids were quite a bit younger than I, and they dressed a little funny, as far as I was concerned.

I purchased a handful of tracts to give away. While walking through the park, I handed a tract to a group of three students. One of them glanced at the tract, crumpled it up and threw it on the ground. That really burned me up. I reached down, picked it up, handed it back to him and said, "Hey, man, straighten up and read it, right now, in front of me! . . ."

The kid was obviously shaken. I decided I was going to break through to him; I was going to teach him to respect God. After he had time to read the tract, I asked, "Now, are you ready to receive Christ? Are you ready to do the four steps and respond to it?"

The guy just looked at me dumbfounded, and said: "Hey, man, who are you kidding? Get off my back!"

With that, I grabbed him by the throat and slammed him up against a tree, my voice rising in anger. "Are you ready to receive Christ? Or are you going to burn in hell, punk?"

Scared out of his wits, he responded, "Yeah, man, whatever you want, whatever you want."

I cuffed him on the side of his head a couple of times and told him to kneel down and pray with me.

About that time, one of the Jesus People came out from behind a tree. Shaking his finger in my face, he said, "Hey, man, you're way out of line and you're an embarrassment to the gospel!"

The young man who confronted Ron about his tactics later instructed him over a cup of coffee: "Ron, you need to know the Person of the Spirit. It's the Holy Spirit who convinces people—not your force. It's the Holy Spirit who shines through you with the love of Jesus that makes people respond."

Ron learned what meekness is. He has dedicated his life to sharing the gospel with kids all over the United States and abroad. He is responsible for thousands of young people coming to Christ and turning away from attitudes that would have led them down the same path to crime he had taken.

Meekness is power under control, and there is no true success without it.

4. *"Blessed are those who hunger and thirst for righteousness, for they will be filled"* (v. 6). Jesus did not say here that those who hunger and thirst for *success* are blessed and will be filled. Again, that is the message of our society. You want success? You have to pay the price. You have to want it so much you can taste it. Only then will you know success.

Jesus blessed the person who hungers for righteousness

more than the one who hungers for results. What matters to him most is not whether a plan or an action will work, not whether it will prove to his benefit, but whether or not it is *right*.

This kind of person keeps coming back to the right just as a magnetic compass always seeks north. He hungers and thirsts for righteousness. Although others may *prefer* righteousness, and many people will do right so long as it pays as well as doing wrong, their real hunger and thirst is for the things their society values as marks of success.

Another temptation for the Christian is not crass success as the world views it but success for a good cause. In the name of a Christian cause, people:

- mistreat others or use them
- take advantage of brothers and sisters
- sacrifice their families
- compromise their own integrity
- destroy their health

Because the cause is Christian they imagine their behavior is Christian. That's the great danger of living for a cause. We are not called to a cause. We are called to a Person, the Lord Jesus Christ. We are called to a community of believers.

As my friend, Doug Murren, loves to say, "The church is not a crowd, it is a community." We are not just a bunch of people who gather in one place. We are not even a bunch of people who gather in one place in the interests of the same cause. We are members one of another, bound together by the love and the life of our Lord Jesus Christ.

To the extent that we are people of a cause, we will at some point manipulate people, seek to dominate them, and maneuver for power. To the extent that we are people

of Christ, we will experience an inner longing for what is
right and for what is consistent with love for others.
Sometimes we have to choose what kind of "success" we
want.

5. *"Blessed are the merciful, for they will be shown mercy"*
(v. 7). Mercy relates to action into another's need. Mourning had to do with feeling others' pain; mercy involves
doing something about their pain. Mercy not only cares
but also has the courage to act. Merciful people are not so
ruled by time and schedule that they cannot reach out to
someone in need. People take precedence over accomplishment.

Julia Ward Howe, the author of "The Battle Hymn of the
Republic," once interceded for a citizen with his congressman. The congressman, however, was too busy with
"important affairs of state" to consider the case. "We may
be thankful that, according to the last notice," observed
Julia Ward Howe, *"God* has not yet gotten that high!"

When we get so high that we cannot be merciful to people, we may be a success in the eyes of the people around
us, but we are something much less in the eyes of Jesus.

6. *"Blessed are the pure in heart, for they will see God"*
(v. 8). Pure means unmixed, undiluted, and unpolluted.
Jesus is speaking about having personal integrity and
cleanness of character. As Billy Graham said to the 1988
convention of National Religious Broadcasters, integrity is
"being the same thing in private that we are in public,"
rather than having a secret life we hope no one ever dis-
covers.

Of course, people need privacy, but the "pure in heart"
are moral and ethical both in private and in public. They
value wholesomeness and are what they seem to be.

One of my friends used to sign his correspondence,
"Without Wax" instead of "Sincerely." This looks a little

strange, but the word "sincere" literally means "without wax." The expression comes out of the Roman marketplace where pottery was displayed. In the more unscrupulous shops when a flaw would appear in a pot or bowl, wax was melted and poured into the scar to cover it. It would look perfect to the unpracticed or hurried eye, but when the sun beat on it or the pot was heated over a fire, the wax would melt and the flaw would appear. Sincere (without wax) came to mean actually being what you appear to be. It is a beautiful picture of one who is "pure in heart."

7. *"Blessed are the peacemakers for they will be called sons of God"* (v. 9). A peacemaker is a person committed to preventing and resolving conflict whenever possible. Some people seem to provoke conflict wherever they go. Their idea of success is to divide and conquer, or at least to fight and win.

God's idea of success is not to beat the other fellow or to take advantage of some conflict with him or in him. God's idea is to reconcile people and to create peace as much as possible. Douglas MacArthur led the Allies to total victory over Japan in World War II, but his greater success was in making friends for the United States out of these former enemies. Defeated enemies have a way of rising again or they remain as troubled, subject peoples. Neither of these situations represents success as much as peacemaking does.

The peacemaker is one who does not nurture conflict, either between people or within them. He is the opposite of a troublemaker; he is a haven for those torn by conflict and a healer to the wounded.

At a particularly painful time in our lives, Barbara and I needed both a haven and a healer. Knowing really nothing about our circumstances, a friend, Dr. Emery Nester, called me from Honolulu. He had recently moved his psychology practice to Hawaii from Portland, where we had come to know him several years before.

"Jerry, I don't know what you and Barb are going through right now," Emery said, "and you don't have to tell me. I just want you to know that I have a small suite in a downtown Honolulu office building. There is a sink, a restroom, and a couch that makes into a bed. If you two can get here, you can spend as many nights as you need in that office, just so you are out each morning in time for my first appointment. Should you want to talk with me, I will give you any time I have."

As much as we needed to get away, we simply had no money to pay for the trip. My heart attack and surgery, combined with the complications and sickness that had taken me to Colorado for more than two months of treatment and therapy, had wiped us out financially. Our church and even our denomination had been generous. Without their help we would really have been destitute. I remember hanging up the phone and crying.

One of our friends heard of Emery's offer and paid Barb's airfare to Honolulu. I told her I would come as soon as I could get the money together. I was able to join her about ten days later. True to his word, Emery gave us his office and his time. He and his wife, Mary Ann, provided us a safe haven: a place where we could find peace, regain hope, and receive the courage to go on with whatever the future held. To us, these friends who came to our aid in a very troubled time in our lives were peacemakers, healers to the wounded, true children of God, and real successes.

8. *"Blessed are those who are persecuted because of righteousness, for theirs is the kingdom of heaven"* (v. 10). Those who crave success, wrongfully understood, often devote themselves to a cynical pursuit of it with little concern for

principle. Jesus reverses that; he calls "blessed" or truly successful the person who for principle will suffer abuse and loss if necessary. In his willingness to lose his life, such a person will find it, Jesus said.

Truly successful people have a life-threatening commitment to something bigger than they are. This isn't a commitment to just anything; their commitment is to righteousness.

I said earlier that our values and not our emotions must control our lives. Our values, in turn, need to be God's values as Jesus described them in the Beatitudes and elsewhere, not the values generally espoused by our culture. Nothing—no achievement, no performance, no recognition—constitutes success if it violates God's values. Similarly, nothing constitutes success that omits these values either. True success involves making God's values our own.

Do not imagine that I am saying that we should make the Beatitudes into our personal code of ethics. That is not my point. Religious systems are concerned with commands, creeds, and codes; those who are religious try to measure up to these standards. By contrast, Christianity is not our trying to live up to God's expectations; it is God at work in us. The Beatitudes are an outline of God's agenda for our lives. Thus, this "Beatitude person" is not someone we're trying to be; it is a description of the person Christ is releasing us to be. Our part is simply to respond to what the Spirit of God is doing in our lives rather than to inhibit him.

Rather than running away from the Captain Bills and other hurting people who come into my life, I must follow that growing inner urge that draws me toward them. I must heed my growing distaste for materialism and distrust of personal power. I must respond to the gentle pressure that pushes me away from a "cause" and toward the Person of

Christ. Those simple things—unexpected urges to help, sudden tears of compassion, small gestures of caring—are it! The kingdom comes. The Spirit of God brings his values into my life, and my part is to answer, "Yes, Lord, that's the kind of success I want."

12

Still More about Success

S uccess is not just a destination; it is also the quality of our journey with God. Success is not just wealth, power, fame, status, or material abundance; it is allowing the Holy Spirit to make God's values ours. These are things I've learned about success, and there is one more. Success is not just grand achievement; it is also living day to day by faith.

SUCCESS AND GRAND ACHIEVEMENT

We have a small problem in the way we relate to outstanding people and great Bible characters. Certainly we are supposed to learn from them and model our lives after them to some extent. But I ask you, how many of us can be a Moses or a Joseph or a David?

Take Moses, for example. He was the great lawgiver and the deliverer of his people. When I think of emulating Moses, I am inclined to think of being great, as he was. His story is particularly enchanting because he was initially rejected. The taunt in his ears after he first tried to fulfill his destiny was, "Who made you ruler and judge over us?" (Exod. 2:14). Joseph, too, was rejected and hated by his brothers. Yet Joseph's dream that his brothers would bow down to him was eventually fulfilled. David was a simple shepherd boy, ridiculed by his brothers when he came down to the battlefront and wanted to withstand Goliath, but he ended up as Israel's great hero and king.

Now here we come along, and we hear these stories. They were written for our admonition, we are told. So what do we do? We either disassociate ourselves and say, "Oh, no, I could never be great like them." Or we imagine that we will someday be great like them, even though no one appreciates us now; we think, "See, they weren't appreciated either."

Both responses miss the mark. Moses, Joseph, and David were types of our Lord Jesus Christ, who was rejected by his own but was destined to be exalted and acknowledged at last as Lord. Moses, Joseph, and David were not types of you and me in this regard; we are not necessarily destined for ultimate greatness as they were. Two million or more Israelites came out of Egypt in the Exodus; each one could not be a Moses. Similarly, there was room for only one Joseph and one David in their respective generations.

If success requires grand achievement, it is for the very few. Take a closer look at Moses. Hebrews describes him as follows:

By faith Moses, when he had grown up, refused to be known as the son of Pharaoh's daughter. He chose to be mistreated along with the people of God rather than to enjoy the pleasures of sin for a short time. He regarded disgrace for the sake of Christ as of greater value than the treasures of Egypt, because he was looking ahead to his reward. By faith he left Egypt, not fearing the king's anger; he persevered because he saw him who is invisible. By faith he kept the Passover and the sprinkling of blood, so that the destroyer of the firstborn would not touch the firstborn of Israel.

By faith the people passed through the Red Sea as on dry land; but when the Egyptians tried to do so they were drowned (Heb. 11:24–29).

Of everything in this account for which Moses is praised, only the last one or perhaps two could be categorized as great achievement. Notice, Moses:

- abandoned the privileges of royalty
- accepted mistreatment
- identified himself with the downtrodden
- renounced temporary, sinful pleasures
- chose disgrace over the treasures of Egypt
- physically left Egypt and all its advantages
- exposed himself to the anger of a powerful king
- brought down plagues upon both Israel and Egypt
- crossed the Red Sea as on dry land

Moses did *all* of these things by faith. When we focus on Moses as a man of great achievement, we miss the point. Great achievements did not make Moses a success. If they did, he would be an example only to that rare person among us who is called to be the Moses (or Joseph or David) of this generation. It was faith that made Moses a success, and it is his faith that is an example to us all.

SUCCESS IS LIVING BY FAITH

This fits perfectly with our earlier observation that success is the quality of the journey, not just its destination. One quality of the journey that identifies us as successful is faith; we are to walk by faith and not by sight. Understanding this makes quite a difference when you stare your own expendability in the face. I thought I was very important—if not indispensable—to the kingdom of God and especially to the church I pastored. It took some doing to cope with the idea that the world and even the kingdom of God could get along quite nicely without me.

I remember commenting to Barb when I was in the hospital, "Why doesn't someone come in here and tell me how terrible things are going at the church without me? There must be something that can't run without my direct supervision." We both laughed; we knew people wanted me to be at ease and not stressed over things unraveling in my absence. I must admit, however, I was a little surprised at how smoothly everything seemed to go.

One thing I've learned now is that success is not buying into the myth of my own indispensability. Success is living by faith in whatever situation I find myself. Maybe, just maybe, that will include great exploits like those of Joseph, Moses, and David. Even if it does, most of my choices of faith will be made in obscurity, as Moses' choices were.

HOW FAITH PLANS FOR TOMORROW

A young man came to my office having been diagnosed with Hodgkin's Disease. He said, "I don't know how to face life now. I don't know how to plan. Should I make close friendships. What about a career?" After we talked for some time, he came to the conclusion that he really had only two choices. He could plan to die, or he could plan to live.

He decided he would plan to live. That was some years ago. He treated the disease with both therapy and prayer, and it went into remission. What a tragedy it would have been had he chosen to plan to die—to see himself as a victim of this disease and interpret life through the fear and pain of Hodgkin's.

Whether we realize it or not, we all face this same decision. We are all planning to die or planning to live. Our mentality as Christians ought to be one of planning to live. This is what eternal life is all about. Eternal life starts now and stretches ahead into infinity; it has no end. In Christ we plan to live forever, starting now.

How we think as we face tomorrow colors everything. If we are planning to die, it means that life is winding down for us. We don't make many plans and investments; we go into a holding pattern. If tomorrow comes, it will be pretty flat and unexciting because we are just waiting to die. I would not call that success. Success means living by faith, not dying by degrees.

WHAT FAITH LOOKS FOR

Faith looks for evidence of God's presence. Anxiety and fear worry about what appears to be evidence of his absence.

One of my doctors was discussing with me the limitations I might face after surgery. "Jerry, don't worry about what you may have lost. Determine to maximize everything you have left."

What a great insight! The thing that made it possible was not my will power, but the fact of the presence of God. I could have looked for evidence that God was absent or angry or indifferent. Among the signs I could have read that way were my heart attack, the subsequent surgery, and the resulting diminished vigor, shortened life expectancy, and general assault on my confidence.

Instead of looking at all those doubt-producing negatives, I chose to look for the evidence that God still lives and loves me. A conversation with a friend who also had had heart surgery and a difficult recovery helped. He asked me, "What valuable things are in your life now that would not be there if you had not had this whole experience?"

It was a fascinating question and one I had not pondered. It prompted me to make a list of the benefits I saw in my life as a direct result of that year of difficulty. I came up with nine big benefits.

1. *My view of life is deeper.* I don't necessarily see more. I do more easily see beyond the veneer of the facts to ponder their meaning and implications.

2. *My pace of life is more balanced —much slower and more deliberate.* I am able to focus on one thing rather than to run on adrenalin through a maze of activities, demands, and expectations. I am less physical and competitive, more relaxed and reflective. I enjoy life more.

3. *My family relationships are richer.* I used to vow in the morning that I would do something with Barb or the boys or with the girls when they were home. Before the day was over, I would be going in so many directions from meetings to hurried study times to appointments that by the time I got home it was either too late or I was too tired to spend much time with the family. The "being laughter" had gone out of my life, as I described in chapter 1.

Through my sickness, the people in my life began to take on significantly more importance than things or duties. I also began to realize how much of the tension we sometimes felt at home was due to my impatience, that is, my disregard for the agenda of another person's life.

In the first months after my surgery, I had to depend on my family to do many things for me that I had always done for myself. It was at times embarrassing to be that weak and to demand so much time and care from other people. But embarrassing or not, a deeper quality of care and love was forged during that time. Happily, our appreciation for one another has continued to this moment.

4. *My values are more clearly defined.* An important question arose during my first days in intensive care. What has been important and has claimed priority in my life up until now? Are those things really the most valuable?

That question continues to engage me to this day. In answering it, I see life more and more in terms of:

- being rather than doing
- relationships rather than tasks
- valuing the moment because there is no guarantee of another

5. *I have a new joy in life and a new peace about death.* Life as I now experience it comes to me in tiny, momentary pieces which can never be repeated or changed. Each moment has importance and value to me, and that sense of valuing each moment releases joy. I am thrilled to be alive! It is not just that I am glad I didn't die; it is that I am more fully living each moment and hour that comes to me.

I am also not afraid of death now. Although I had a valid theology of death and had walked with others to its door, I frankly had not thought much about death as it relates to me. Now I have, and I am at peace about it. This very peace seems to fuel my joy in living.

6. *I have a knowledge and a sense of awe about my own body.* It is a remarkable machine. I will never forget my overwhelming sense of wonder at seeing my own heart beating on the video screen during my first angiogram. That spurred my interest, and I began to ask questions and read as many books as I could about the heart. My purpose was not to become an expert, far from it. I am simply in awe at this body God has created for me to live in, and, if anything, that sense of wonder only continues to grow.

7. *I have received many new tools with which to manage and handle my life.* My intense, competitive, "Type A" personality has had to be dismantled. I have had to learn entirely new ways of dealing with life. That's a big assignment, and it's by no means finished. But I at least know tools exist, and I know something of how to employ them to make life easier for me and the people with whom I work and live.

8. *I have added new dimensions of fellowship without denying or rejecting the old.* When my illness and its subsequent complications forced an end to my almost twenty-year ministry at Gresham, we weren't sure whether there was such a thing as life after East Hill Church or not. East Hill had been our life's work, and Gresham was the only home our children had ever known.

God stepped into our lives at this most crucial time, however, and gave us options we had never imagined. No one has had to take another's place in our lives. We did not have to replace East Hill. Those people have a permanent place in our lives, and we in theirs.

Now we also have our new lives in Seattle. I have a wealth of acceptance, of fulfillment in my work, of *joie de vivre* that I had nearly lost during the difficult and tiring years just before my body went on strike. Our family, too, is content. We have no doubt that God hand-picked our new area, house, cul-de-sac, neighbors, schools, everything, just for us right now.

9. *I have a much greater understanding of pain and suffering, and I think that enriches my work as well as my living.* I have a friend who was in a terrible accident. Her spine was injured, and she is now paralyzed from the neck down, except for the use of her arms and limited use of her hands. She had been an active, athletic person, always ready for the next challenge. I wondered how she could cope with her handicap.

Recently she told me, "I have decided that my life will not be centered around this handicap. There is more to life than coping with a handicap. God can still use me. In fact, what I say now seems to have more impact than before the accident. Perhaps the wheelchair is something God can use in my life."

My friend was not implying that God had caused or blessed the accident. She was saying that because of the presence of God, her life still had meaning and significance. She was looking for God's presence, not his absence. That is faith. For her, as for all of us, that kind of faith spells success.

THE NOBLENESS OF SUCCESS

Here's what we've said about success thus far: Success has to do with the quality of your journey. Success depends on making God's values your own. Success is walking by faith.

That sounds very different from some of the formulas for success you hear these days. I guess it all depends on whose idea of success you want to buy into. Some entertain pretty crass and sub-Christian notions of what success is—the so-called American dream of wealth, power, and pleasure. Thinkers, to say nothing of Christian thinkers, have always known better.

In 1893, Katherine Lee Bates wrote a poem later set to music and known to us as "America the Beautiful." Australians and Canadians sing it with their own nation named instead. The third stanza ends:

America, America, May God thy gold refine
'Til all success be nobleness And every gain divine.

The success that is nobleness—let's you and I aspire to that! Think of nobleness as being like Abraham. Don't think of Abraham when he was rich and powerful. No, I remember an incident that is to this day one of the most obscure recorded episodes of his life.

Lot had gone off to live in Sodom, and, when the forces of Chedorlaomer sacked the city of Sodom, he had been carried away captive. Abraham gathered a rescue force, pursued the army of Chedorlaomer, rescued Lot and the others, and recovered all the loot. In doing so he not only incurred the risk of the operation itself but exposed himself to the very real possibility of future retaliation from Chedorlaomer.

The king of Sodom offered to reward Abraham. "Give me the people and keep the goods for yourself," he said (Gen. 14:21). But Abraham replied, "I have raised my hand to the Lord, God Most High, Creator of heaven and earth, and have taken an oath that I will accept nothing belonging to you, not even a thread or the thong of a sandal, so that you will never be able to say, 'I made Abram rich.'"

Now *that* was nobleness. That was success. And it would have been success if Abraham had never become rich, for success is making a quality journey, internalizing God's values, and living by faith. May this success be abundantly yours!

Part 6

A Few Things I've Learned about Guidance

13

About Guidance

No doubt God intends his children to experience his guidance. To be led of the Spirit is part of our birthright as God's people. The Bible says, "Those who are led by the Spirit of God are sons of God" (Rom. 8:14).

While the principle of divine guidance is not in doubt, many specific applications of the principle are. The questions include:

- What does it mean to be led of the Spirit?
- When and for what do we need divine guidance?
- What should we understand guidance to be?
- How is guidance received?

DOES GOD SCHEDULE LUNCH?

I was meeting with Christian leaders to prepare for a large conference, and the directors wanted to bathe everything in prayer. That was fine, but they also had the idea that we would act only as the Spirit led through prayer. I wasn't quite sure about all this, so I decided to observe as well as participate. I wanted to see just how decisions were made.

I noticed that without exception three individual leaders got all the "guidance." This was about the same thing one would have expected had there been no "waiting on the Lord" for direction.

At one point, one of the three leaders announced, "I think the Lord is saying we ought to break now for lunch." Really, it doesn't take the Lord to say that. I don't think the Lord gave a hoot when we had lunch. Lunch ought to be sometime around noon. I mean, God gave us a brain. We do not need some special leading from God to use our common sense.

The Bible says we are to be "led by the Spirit of God," as we have already noted. However, when we look at the context we learn some interesting things about what being "led by the Spirit" means:

> Therefore, brothers, we have an obligation—but it is not to the sinful nature, to live according to it. For if you live according to the sinful nature, you will die; but if by the Spirit you put to death the misdeeds of the body, you will live, because *those who are led by the Spirit of God are sons of God.* For you did not receive a spirit that makes you a slave again to fear, but you received the spirit of sonship. And by him we cry, "Abba, Father." The Spirit himself testifies with our spirit that we are God's children (Rom. 8:12–16, emphasis added).

Working back up through this passage, we find several critically important concepts about guidance:

1. *Guidance begins with understanding who we are.* God wants to tell you and me something a lot more important than when we should break for lunch. He wants to tell us we are his children. The Spirit "testifies with our spirit that we are God's children" (v. 16).

The verb "testifies" is in a continuous present tense in the original language. It means God is always saying that. If you are led of the Lord—if you hear what he is saying to you at any given moment—it will be a reaffirmation in some form that you really are his child. You are not necessarily what you think you are or what others say about you, but you are God's child.

It's crucially important that we hear God speak this message to our hearts. As the passage says, if we hear the Spirit testifying that we are God's children, we will have "the spirit of sonship" (v. 15). Our lives will be characterized by a loving father-child relationship with God. By contrast, the same verse tells us, in the absence of this sense of our sonship, we live with "a spirit that makes you a slave again to fear."

We need to ask ourselves which spirit animates our lives. Do we serve God because we are his children and it's the most natural thing in the world? Or do we accommodate God because we are afraid of what will happen if we don't? That isn't really serving God at all; it is serving (or being a slave to) our own fear.

To be led of the Spirit, then, is to hear God say we are his children and to respond, "Abba, Father." This spirit of sonship is a healing balm that gets much of the twistedness out of us. No longer slaves to fear, we are freed to live in liberty as children of God.

2. *Guidance always leads toward holiness of life.* Those who are led by the Spirit of God are people who "by the Spirit put to death the misdeeds of the body" (v. 13). Do you want to know the will of God for your life? Here it is: Clean up your act! "Oh, but I need to know whether I should be a preacher or a mechanic, live in middle America or the third world, study biblical languages or psychology." No, you need to clean up your life. You will be out of the will of God in any vocation, in any country, with any skills as long as you are dominated by sin.

One of the major problems Christians have in seeking guidance is that we often persist in asking the wrong

questions. The group of praying leaders I described earlier
did not need guidance about when to eat lunch; we
needed guidance to live righteously, peacefully, and joyfully and to communicate this life to those coming to the
conference. As Scripture says, "The kingdom of God is not
a matter of eating and drinking, but of righteousness,
peace and joy in the Holy Spirit" (Rom. 14:17).

Someone says, "You mean it doesn't matter where we
live or what our vocation is as long as we are good Christians?" I'm not quite saying that; it may matter very much.
What I am saying is that the more crucial issue is to be
God's person through and through first; the other questions will be answered without great difficulty then.

THE "GUIDANCE" THAT PARALYZES

The Christian life becomes for some a guilt-filled, anxious,
apprehensive way that leads to virtual paralysis. They are
afraid to do anything because they aren't sure the Lord is
leading them, and they don't want to make a mistake or
get out of the will of God.

> "Is there sin in my life?"
> "Have I repented enough?"
> "Have I prayed enough?"
> "Should I have fasted?" Or if I did fast, "Should I
> have fasted longer?"
> "Am I acting in the energy of the flesh?"
> "Is my own ego involved in this?"

On and on it goes. The subtle thing is that it all sounds
so spiritual. Surely these are concerns we should have, are
they not? Perhaps. Although these are questions that
sometimes need to be asked and answered, they are not
the right focus. They orient us toward ourselves and our

performance rather than toward God and our relationship
with him.

What I call the "relationship concept of guidance" is
found not only in the Romans 8 passage we already examined but also in Psalm 37. Most of the early verses of this
psalm begin with a verb. Each one identifies something
the people of God are to do or not do. Yet these key words
are mostly relational; the only performance-oriented verbs
describe things God's people are *not* supposed to do, as
italicized in the following list:

> *"Do not fret"* (v. 1).
> "Trust in the Lord" (v. 3).
> "Delight yourself in the Lord" (v. 4).
> "Commit your way to the Lord" (v. 5).
> "Be still before the Lord" (v. 7).
> *"Refrain from anger"* (v. 8).

In the context, the people addressed here are those who
"will inherit the land" (v. 9). The land was not just a piece
of geography. It was the place where God and his people
would dwell together. The land was the symbol of a
covenant relationship.

In the middle of the chapter is a beautiful description of
what it means to experience God's guidance: "The Lord
delights in the way of the man whose step he has made
firm; though he stumble, he will not fall, for the Lord up-
holds him with his hand" (vv. 23–24).

This psalm begins with an admonition not to fret
"because of evildoers." "Fret" means to be anxious or
uptight. To want God's guidance is good; to be anxious
and uptight about finding God's will is not good. Again in
verse 8, we read, "Do not fret—it leads only to evil."

You see, Christ's endeavor in our lives is always toward

freedom. "It is for freedom that Christ has set us free" (Gal. 5:1). Our understanding of guidance must lead us into freedom and not into bondage.

THE TARGET THEORY

One concept of guidance that consistently leads to anxiety and paralysis is the target theory. Think of God's perfect will as the bull's-eye. The next ring out represents God's conditional will and the next his permissive will. If your action falls anywhere outside those three circles, you've missed the target completely and are out of the will of God.

Some imagine this is taught in Romans 12 where we read about the "good, and acceptable, and perfect will" of God (v. 2, KJV). As the Sears catalog once offered three grades of products labeled "good," "better," and "best," so there is God's good will, and, in ascending order of value, his acceptable will and his perfect will.

What a formula for anxiety! If you want to make God's will something to fret about, just try to figure out exactly what God's perfect will is so you can hit the bull's-eye every time. Actually, "good" and "acceptable" and "perfect" are not degrees at all; God's will is all three of these at the same time.

Don't fret about finding God's "perfect" will; it is self-defeating. It's like getting all upset trying to find peace. You're getting out of God's will by the way you're seeking to know God's will.

Can you accept that? Can you give yourself permission to relax? Can you trust and delight in the Lord, commit your way to him and be still, as Psalm 37 says? Sometimes we feel that if we are not a little uptight, we are not serious about following the Lord. We begin to feel like the whole kingdom of God rests on our decisions.

How egotistical! Give yourself and the rest of us a break. Stop fretting! The kingdom of God will not rise or fall on your performance. You can't make a mistake big enough to destroy God's kingdom. I'm not saying that in order to give you license or because your actions and attitudes are unimportant. It is just the opposite. I am saying it to release you, to free you from the paralysis of fear so that you can act.

HOW GUIDANCE FLOWS FROM RELATIONSHIP

Psalm 37 begins with a don't ("don't fret"), but it quickly moves on to what we should do. "Trust in the Lord and do good" (v. 3). Usually the will of the Lord lies plainly before us. You want to know what you should do? It's simple: do good.

A remarkable example of guidance comes to us from Samuel's message to Saul, as recorded in 1 Samuel 10. Samuel described in great detail what would happen to Saul:

When you leave me today, you will meet two men near Rachel's tomb, at Zelzah on the border of Benjamin. They will say to you, "The donkeys you set out to look for have been found. And now your father has stopped thinking about them and is worried about you. He is asking, 'What shall I do about my son?'"

Then you will go on from there until you reach the great tree of Tabor. Three men going up to God at Bethel will meet you there. One will be carrying three young goats, another three loaves of bread, and another a skin of wine. They will greet you and offer you two loaves of bread, which you will accept from them.

After that you will go to Gibeah of God, where there is a Philistine outpost. As you approach the town, you will meet a procession of prophets coming down from the high place with lyres, tambourines, flutes, and harps being played before them, and they will be prophesying. The Spirit of the Lord will come upon you in power, and you will prophesy with them; and you will be changed into a different person. Once these signs are fulfilled, do whatever your hand finds to do, for God is with you (vv. 2–7).

The first several verses describe the kind of guidance we dream about. Specific details of whom we will meet and where, what they will do and say, and how we are to respond. Wow! That's dramatic! But what's this we read at the end? After all these remarkable signs are fulfilled, instead of expecting the same sort of thing to continue, Saul is told to "do whatever your hand finds to do."

Saul became a different person when the Spirit of the Lord came upon him. The unspiritual Saul had remarkable signs to guide him for a while, but the Spirit-led Saul didn't need sign guidance. Why? "For God is with you" (v. 7).

God is with us also if we have received Christ as Savior and been filled with the Holy Spirit. We don't need signs to know his will. We need simply to trust in the Lord and do good. We need to be content to follow the Lord one step at a time, content with the assurance that we will always know enough to make the next right move by faith.

AN ENORMOUS ELEMENT OF JOY

The next guideline in Psalm 37 says, "Delight yourself in the Lord and he will give you the desires of your heart" (v. 4). We think, "Do you mean that if I delight myself in the Lord he will give me whatever I want?" That idea is implied in the text, but essentially we are being told rather that God will initiate or sponsor appropriate desires in our hearts. The thing we desire will be what he has prompted.

"Delight" is an intimate, relational word. It's a word we might use to characterize a relationship between lovers. It's warm, uncalculating, and effusive. It has about it an enormous element of joy and nothing of strain, effort, or demand. It suggests a situation in which two people thoroughly enjoy each other and want the moment to continue forever. When you fellowship with the Lord this way, your heart begins to beat in harmony with his. Some desires begin to grow in you, and they are his desires as well.

Ordinarily we are suspicious of our desires. When I was a kid I thought I didn't dare tell God what I wanted because he'd see that I didn't get it. If he knew something I didn't want to do, that's what he would require of me. Even humans are better than a God like that. We don't deny people whatever they want just to be spiteful. We also understand that people will be happier and do a better job working at something they like. God is at least as smart and as good as humans. He plants desires in our hearts if we love him, and those desires are legitimate and good. To put it another way, your "huncher" got saved along with you, so don't be afraid to follow your hunches.

To keep out of the paralysis that comes with faulty ideas of guidance, I generally assume a green light until I get a red one. Otherwise, I could sit at one of life's intersections all day and accomplish nothing. If I want to do something legitimate, I go ahead and do it. If it's not God's will, he has effective ways of getting my attention. Of course, I'm talking about a situation where I want to do God's will, not one in which I have a rebellious or willful attitude.

MAKING OUR DESIRES COME TO PASS

I believe God has given me certain desires. I assume I have a green light in pursuing these desires, and I move in that direction. I also refer the entire process to his constant supervision: "Commit your way to the Lord; trust in him" (Ps. 37:5).

I say, "OK, Lord, how is this going to work out?" I don't know how to get from desire to the actualizing of desire. That's one reason I keep a journal, so I can see the pattern of God's working in my life. I note a prayer on one side of the page, then go back a few weeks later to see what's been happening. I record the results on the other side of the page. It's surprising how much he brings to pass as I commit my way to him. If I don't see "results," that's OK, too. I've learned that my timing is not the same as his, and if I don't get my desires right away, that's not a matter of life and death.

"Be still before the Lord and wait patiently for him" (v. 7). There's no need to complain or worry. Delight in the Lord, enjoy him, and be patient. He brings things together when it's right. My desire may be a tiny part of some much larger thing God is doing. He alone has the big picture.

WHEN GUIDANCE DOESN'T WORK OUT AS EXPECTED

"Refrain from anger and turn from wrath" (v. 8). This is an interesting verse because the last part says what to do when you've failed to do the first part. To "turn from wrath" would not be necessary if we refrained from anger in the first place.

God knows that sometimes we do get angry, even with him. He is not intimidated by our anger. He wants us to deal with it rather than to deny it, to turn from it when we haven't been able to refrain from it.

I was angry with God when our church in Gresham experienced explosive growth. I had gone to Gresham with the belief that I would be left alone to minister to a few people in a small town and would not have to contend with the hassles of a big church. One comment made to me was, "You're going to bury yourself in that dusty little town, and no one will ever hear from you again."

That was exactly what I wanted, and I took the words as a prophecy from God. My choice wasn't from lack of vision on my part so much as from a sense of inferiority. I was convinced that I was small time and not cut out for a big church.

Things didn't work out as I expected. The church began to grow and then to mushroom. All kinds of people began attending, including some drug addicts and counterculture types who scared me to death.

At one point the church grew from 500 to 1800 in just the few weeks between New Year's and Easter. The biggest church I'd ever attended was 350 people. I didn't know what was happening or what I should do other than just grab a chunk of the boat and hope I made it to shore.

I remember the day I paused, tired, and said, "God, you double-crossed me. You called me up here to invest my life in a few people and now look. I haven't the foggiest idea what to do, and I'm scared even to go to church." God did not go off into a corner and pout. Instead, I had the distinct impression that he patted me on the head. That insulted me even more. But he was saying to me, "I will work with you on the basis of who I know you to be, not on a basis of who you think you are."

So much of what we call guidance is like that; it is a replacing of our views with his. In fact a pretty good definition would be "guidance is getting God's viewpoint." Getting God's viewpoint is crucially important, otherwise we could not interpret life when the going gets tough— which it often does. In fact, when we involve ourselves in the broader purposes of God, things seldom go as we think they should. If we see our personal expectations and the will of God as synonymous, we are bound to become both discouraged and confused.

We need a concept of guidance that will not betray us when disappointments and seeming failures come, when our personal expectations are not met. Even when it appears that a disaster has taken place, we must not put a period to what is really an incomplete sentence. We must keep walking, keep on responding from God's heart. Ultimately, his fingerprints will be seen clearly on the finished page. I'll illustrate and explain more fully what I mean in the next chapter.

14

More about Guidance

Sometimes when guidance doesn't work out as we expect, we begin to second-guess our decisions. The worse the situation becomes, the more likely we are to doubt the wisdom of our choices. We may also become confused about the whole question of how to know God's will, since we thought we knew it, but things went sour for us.

As one Christian college president said upon being fired from his post, "I came here in obedience to the call of God. If the board is right in firing me and it's not God's will that I be here, then I don't know how to find God's will." He was genuinely confused about the events and remained so for years.

I have been involved in a few puzzling and difficult situations myself. I believed I was doing God's will once, but the project I led my church into, after costing untold hours of work and nearly half a million dollars, did not end up as I anticipated. At many points along the way, it felt like a mistake and even a failure.

What is one to do in such circumstances? Two options are apparent:

1. You can decide you were wrong even though you conscientiously sought God's guidance all along

the way. If you take this path, it is likely to shake your confidence in God or, at least, in your ability to find and do God's will. You could spend the rest of your life cowering in the shadows, afraid because you know your best efforts to follow God may result only in disaster.

2. You can insist you were right in your decision and refuse to fold your sails now just because there are contrary winds. If you take this course, you may plunge stubbornly ahead against all evidence that things are bad and getting worse. Real tragedies are made of such attitudes. This is the mentality of madmen, who lead their followers to destruction rather than alter the course.

Both of the options described above have a problem. They are static and backward looking. We need to see the will of God in terms of an ongoing or unfolding process. Making adjustments in midstream is not equivalent to saying we have heretofore missed God's will. Rather it can be an embracing of a new and unanticipated direction God has chosen to go. We must remember that we are always in a response position to God. He is not in a response position to us. He is both the beginning and the end. He knows where we have been, where we are, and where we are going. Quite frankly, we don't see any of these accurately. This is one reason we need the Lord; we are extremely short-sighted.

It also should be said in regard to option two that perseverance *is* a Christian virtue, and we certainly cannot decide whether God is directing us down a certain path by the presence or lack of difficulties we encounter. Clearly we need to distinguish between God-inspired persistence and ego-inspired stubbornness. This line is not so easily drawn as one may think.

Foundational to any understanding of guidance is our integrity before God. Integrity requires an open mind and a soft heart toward God, and toward trusted friends and associates. On the one hand, to bull ahead in order to prove ourselves right is a sure route to disaster. On the other, to persist in the face of criticism, difficulty, and opposition with the assurance of God's strength and the honest support of godly associates is necessary in any kingdom endeavor.

To illustrate the points I've been making, let me tell you the story of "New Life USA."

A CALL TO ACTION

I had been speaking at a pastors' conference near Manila when I was invited to Hong Kong to a gathering of national leaders from five Asian countries. At the time, refugees were fleeing Cambodia in any boat or barge they could find. They were inundating Hong Kong by the thousands, homeless and sick.

I walked through the refugee camps that had sprung up everywhere, even in parking garages. I saw children playing in the smelly mud, some even drinking from the open sewer water running down between the paper shacks and makeshift shelters. There seemed to be a glazed, painful look in every eye. Hundreds of children had been orphaned by the war or the hardship of the boat trip. They were adopted by anybody who happened to be handy and compassionate. The terms "refugee" and "orphan" took on new meaning for me.

I remember standing in the middle of all this and saying, "I must do something besides look. I must act in response to this pain in some way." Even as I write this now, those faces and eyes leap back into focus. They are permanently etched on my memory.

The Scripture says, "If anyone has material possessions

and sees his brother in need but has no pity on him, how can the love of God be in him? Dear children, let us not love with words or tongue but with actions and in truth" (1 John 3:17–18). The same kind of conviction moved me there in Hong Kong, and I determined to do something in the face of this extreme need.

The Plan Develops

When I got back home, I described to our congregation what I had seen. I told them of my resolve to act. I remember stating, "It would take a town even to begin to house and help a significant number of these people."

We began to pray as a congregation, asking God to direct us as to how we should respond. Then one of our men discovered a town for sale! About a hundred miles east of us was a former military base, now abandoned. It included over twenty houses with two or three bedrooms each, large barracks, a commercial kitchen with a large dining room, a shop, a gymnasium, even a bowling alley, plus numerous other buildings, equipment, and facilities. It was also an incorporated town!

Our church leadership and the entire congregation sensed God's direction and blessing as we planned to purchase the town and convert it to a facility to receive refugees and give them the skills to adapt to American culture. Soon the larger community beyond our own congregation caught sight of this vision as well. Donations of food, clothing, and furniture poured in. People contacted us who were willing to move to the base and invest their lives and resources in what we were doing. Many had valuable job and professional skills needed for our effort. New Life USA was born. We were off on a great adventure.

The farmers and business people of Condon, the nearest town to the base, were curious and naturally a little suspicious of us at first. Many came to see for themselves what was going on. Later, after the first refugees arrived, the farmers hired any who wanted to earn extra money and paid them in cash at the end of each day.

More and more refugees arrived. The stories of what they had suffered were pure horror. It was not unusual to see a young couple with more children than could possibly have been born to them. Many were orphans who had been informally adopted after their parents died or were killed. Now we were in a position to act in a significant way to see that their long ordeal was over. New Life USA was a reality.

The Gathering Storm

Then came unforeseen problems. Tim Peterson, who was directly responsible for New Life USA, recounts:

> Since, ultimately, the state had to assume responsibility for refugees . . . they were naturally involved in the process. What we didn't know at first was that the personnel were extremely hostile toward "religious do-gooders" (which they wrongly assumed we were) and were predetermined that we would fail and thereby prove the point that we were unfit to try to do something new that was not consistent with their viewpoint.

> The state would not accept our plan to create a microcosm on the base and train the people there in skills that would help them assimilate into society. Instead they required us to take the refugees to the neighboring town of Condon to be trained in consumer education there. The key state leader actually told me that we were expected to take the adult members into the bars and introduce them to the American practices of smoking and drinking.

The struggle with all of this political pressure increased until it felt like we were being thwarted at every turn in simply bringing help, healing, and hope to these people who had suffered so much. Meanwhile, the number of refugees being allowed into the country declined. Our costs were extremely high and going higher because of the inflation and high interest rates then gripping the United States.

We could read the handwriting on the wall and began plans to move our operation into Portland and scale it down. Then came what seemed at the time a crushing blow. I could hardly believe the "news" story on television. We were accused of keeping refugees against their will in a wired fortress and using them virtually as slave labor to achieve our own ends.

As I sat watching that telecast, I felt victimized and defeated. It seemed that all our hard work and sacrifice for those people had been flushed right down the drain. I felt pain for the many church members and friends who had sacrificed so much for so long. Staring blankly at the television set, I said to my associate, "Well, Don, it's all over. That's the end of New Life USA."

But the story was far from over. In fact, this particular chapter was not yet ended. I couldn't see that then. I was hurt, confused, angry, and disappointed. I did what we often do at such times; I put a period to God's unfinished sentence.

Actually, the hostile intentions of those who planted the news story failed totally. Their purpose was to discredit our work, undermine our reputation, and put us out of business. None of these things happened in the long run. Several things they did not anticipate happened instead.

1. The story of what we were doing spread broadly as the number of news items about New Life USA exploded in every paper throughout our state and beyond. Most of those stories were written from interviews with me or from news releases we issued. They were for the most part favorable. The original television attack did not hit the United Press International or Associated Press news wires.

Many of the interviews and follow-up stories did and were covered favorably.

2. There was no indication that our support sagged. In fact, mail and donation response increased. When we moved the operation to Portland from Condon, we had more furniture and clothing than we could handle. We hired people full time just to size and sort donated clothing. An entire barn was filled and kept full of furniture even though we made deliveries every day of furniture and equipment to refugee families.

3. The very people and agencies that opposed us in the beginning ended up referring refugees to us for help, studying how we operated, and incorporating our methods.

4. Agency leaders came to us and expressed their admiration for our work as well as the way we handled the entire "news" episode. They were shocked when they saw us responding with love and openness toward our avowed enemies, rather than suing or reacting with vengeance and anger. In the agency community, the project came to be seen for what it really was—an outpouring of love to homeless people, with no strings attached.

The entire episode was a clear example of "not fretting because of evildoers." Our people spent no time getting back at anyone. They gave themselves to their mission without interruption. They cared for the poor, fed the hungry, and gave homes to the homeless. East Hill Church became a good example of a congregation of Christians acting on the basis of its values.

WHAT HAPPENED TO OUR GUIDANCE?

The question posed before I told about New Life USA was this: How do you react when the thing you thought God led you into does not work out according to your expectations? Do you decide you misread God's will . . . and become confused or cynical about the whole question of guidance? Do you stubbornly fight on, closing your eyes to reality in order to maintain the claim that God led you?

I said there was another option, and it's illustrated by New Life USA. That option is neither to renounce the original leading nor stick stubbornly to the original plan. It is to continue by adjusting yourself to the new realities and humbly seeking God's wisdom as you go. This means you must not be eaten up by hand wringing over mistakes you may have made along the way. You must not second-guess everything you have done and thereby become paralyzed and incapable of any further decisive action. Neither can you be unresponsive to continued guidance along the way.

In the case of New Life USA, we closed the base but continued to work intensively with refugees in the greater Portland area, where our church was located. We continued teaching English, placing refugees in training programs, and finding them jobs. We gave furniture, household goods, and clothing freely to anyone in the refugee community who needed it. We provided transportation, taught driving, and generally served as a resource for whatever needs we could meet. We did all these things with no strings attached.

Some refugees began asking about Jesus and our church. One of our base staff members, Ron Smith, was a former missionary to Thailand who spoke the refugees' language fluently, so he began teaching them the Scriptures in their own language.

I remember the Sunday morning we baptized the first Asian converts. There was a long line of people, of all ages, from boys and girls old enough to understand the Gospel to elderly men and women who were turning from the animism and superstition of their past. We listened in awe, and we wept as we heard the stories of how they had come to Christ.

How Do We Finally Decide?

Were we in the will of God when we developed New Life USA? I believe the answer to that is definitely yes. With the hindsight of years, however, that question could be answered differently, depending on how you interpret the data.

A list of reasons could be cited for believing that God never intended us to do what we did. These might include:

1. It did not pan out as we had envisioned it.
2. It depleted our financial resources as a church, creating a ripple effect of difficulties and curtailing ministry in other areas.
3. It absorbed literally thousands of hours of time and effort that proved to be "wasted in a lost cause."

I can also give a list of reasons for taking the view that we were led of God. It's interesting that my reasons accommodate the same data as on the preceding list, just viewed differently.

1. The fulfillment of our expectations is not a valid test of whether an action is in the will of God. This has been one of my major points all along, and if it's not yet established, I trust it will be before we're through.

2. It may seem that New Life USA drained off money from the church. Yet to say that it did so betrays a misunderstanding of what the church is all about. It did delay construction of certain physical facilities. That was in line with our values as a congregation. Saving the lives of people (in this case Asian refugees) *is* the ministry of the church. Buildings are not. Ultimately the buildings were constructed, but not at the expense of loving and caring for people in need.

3. Hundreds of people were given the opportunity to pour out their hearts, their abilities, and their resources in love to people who would never remember their names and never be able to repay them—or for that matter even say thanks in most cases. If that was a waste, it was like the alabaster box of precious ointment poured out on Jesus' feet. It was a waste to critical (and crooked) bystanders, but it was praiseworthy in the eyes of Jesus (see John 12:1–7).

Also germane to how we should look at this outpouring of love is what the Apostle Paul said to the Christians at Philippi when they had sent him a money gift. Paul thanked them warmly and then added, "I am not saying this because I am in need, for I have learned to be content whatever the circumstances." Why then was their giving so gratifying? "But I am looking for what may be credited to your account" (Phil. 4:11, 17). To give from motives of love is beautiful in the eyes of God whether it actually meets desperate needs or not. In the case of New Life USA, literally hundreds of people with desperate needs were helped significantly.

I could cite many more reasons to believe God led us to reach out to refugees in what became New Life USA:

1. God's grace flowed through many lives as people gave without expectation of return, as just described.
2. People were helped: families were reunited, lives were saved, destitute people were given physical necessities plus the skills needed to survive in a new land.
3. Individuals came to know Christ. I described earlier the joy I experienced when a whole group of new believers from among the refugee community was baptized. This happened many times.

4. Many people were channeled into new and significant ministries. I think of one young couple in particular. After we'd moved New Life USA back to Portland, they located their family inside the Asian community in order to establish a beachhead for the gospel right in the midst of the darkness, suspicion, and superstition. Today they are effective and productive missionaries in Japan. Three other staff families are now in overseas mission service.

5. We were enabled to respond to a critical need in another world trouble spot. A Christian, General Efrain Rios Montt, had become president of strife-torn Guatemala. He knew of George Hughes, our director of New Life USA, from years before when George had helped rebuild Guatemala City after an earthquake. Rios Montt asked George to return to spearhead a project to alleviate the suffering in outlying mountain villages decimated by guerrilla warfare. It was a window in time, a brief period when we could get in and out and save many lives. Our response mechanism was already in place: New Life USA. Not only did we send George but also teams of people and critical supplies.

6. We were obedient to the principles of God's word. Frankly, I don't think we need dramatic guidance to do what Christ has already told us to do. Feed the hungry, clothe the naked, open our arms to the homeless—these are expected responses from those who know the love of Christ.

If you saw someone struck down in the street by a hit-and-run driver, would you need guidance before going out to help? Jesus wasn't pleased with a priest and a Levite who passed by a wounded man in the street, but he commended the Samaritan who stopped to help (see Luke 10:29–37). Maybe the priest and the Levite were praying for guidance, I don't know. What I do know is that they should have acted.

Understand, I am not saying we made no mistakes in regard to New Life USA, for we certainly did. I'm not saying we knew what we were getting into, for in many respects we did not. Nevertheless, I believe our basic response was of God. The total impact of that enterprise will be known only in eternity.

GETTING DOWN TO BASICS

It's a matter of little concern whether you praise or criticize me in the case of New Life USA. What matters is whether you and I come to sound concepts regarding guidance.

Much has been written about how to determine God's will. We need to have obedient hearts, honestly desiring to do his will. We need to pray and ask for wisdom. We need to consider the counsel of godly people. We need to check everything against the teaching of God's word. All this is fine, excellent in fact, but we also need to be sure we recognize some underlying basics.

1. *Our concept of guidance is controlled by our ideas of what constitutes success.* In the case of New Life USA, the questions raised about whether or not we were in the will of God revolved around the seeming failure of the mission. That's typical. We think, "If it didn't succeed in the ways we expected or thought it should, obviously God wasn't in it."

A businessman asked me recently, "How can I get God to bless my business?"

I replied, "What would you call God's blessing in your business?" He looked at me as if I had suddenly become brain dead.

"I've tithed regularly," he said. "I try to live by the

golden rule in relationships with my customers. I'm doing everything I can think of to do. But my business is going further and further in the hole. It looks as though I may go bankrupt."

"So making money and not going bankrupt would to your mind be God's blessing, is that right?" I asked.

"Of course. God certainly doesn't want me to go bankrupt."

"Are you sure God is as committed to the American dream as you are?" That started a long conversation about what really is important in life, why he was serving God in the first place, what God's values are, and how those values relate to our lives.

To assume that God is as interested in our financial well-being as most of us are in this greedy and materialistic culture simply is not valid. God uses very different measurements from ours. He is concerned with our heart, attitudes, relationships, eternity. I have absolutely no doubt that God would sacrifice all our stuff to save us— and he would do it without even blinking. So, then, we will have trouble finding God's guidance for our decisions and even more trouble correctly interpreting what flows from those decisions if we are not plugged into God's agenda, which in turn is determined by God's values.

2. *Guidance is impossible when God becomes a means to our ends.* Many people confuse their Christian faith. They see Jesus and his salvation as a means to an end. Having faith or giving money or being spiritual become means by which they manipulate God and force him to come through for them. For some, even worship is a means to an end. Not all that long ago it was popular in some circles to believe that all we had to do when trouble came was praise our way out of it.

When we get confused in this way, we lose the ability to understand guidance. We ask the wrong questions, so how in the world will we ever find the right answers? Jesus is not the means to anything. He *is* the end. We don't worship him in order to get something from him. We worship him because he is worthy of worship.

To understand Christianity as essentially a means by which we get what we believe our needs are is tragic. God in Jesus Christ came to provide a way to forgive our sins. We then could be related to God as Father and be brought into alignment with his design and intended purposes. There's a wide gulf between our being brought into alignment with his purposes and his being used for ours.

Jesus taught his disciples to pray: "Our Father in heaven, hallowed be your name, your kingdom come, your will be done" (Matt. 9:9–10). So long as we try to use God to satisfy our needs and wishes, the real prayer of our hearts is, "My will be done," regardless of the words we mouth.

There is no doubt that when we are brought into right relationship with God through trusting in Jesus Christ, we experience healing, deliverance, and a radical change for the better at the very core of our lives. Sometimes that feels good, gives us peace, and makes our lives go smoothly. At other times it hurts, throws our lives into chaos, strains our relationships, and upsets our comfortable plans.

A charming exchange between Mr. Beaver and Lucy in C. S. Lewis's children's story *The Lion, the Witch and the Wardrobe* makes the point. They are talking about the great lion, Aslan, who is the Christ figure throughout the book. Lucy asks, "But is he safe?" "Of course he is not safe," answers Mr. Beaver, "but he is good."

Jesus Christ is not safe. When we invite him into our hearts and lives, everything is placed in jeopardy. Our values are challenged. Our easy answers for difficult questions are no longer satisfactory. Our points of security and even our plans for the future are in serious danger. Our comfort, pleasure, and the American dream can no longer determine our life's direction and goals. He is not safe, but he is good!

Those who distort Christianity into a means of satisfying their own needs and wants are trying to make a pet out of Aslan the lion. They have become users instead of worshipers. With this kind of twisted thinking, guidance becomes simply an expedient for tapping into God's wisdom to give them an edge in reaching their goals.

The problem is, God isn't playing that game. User Christians typically end up frustrated and confused. They are hopelessly adrift in terms of true guidance, and they often are heard to complain, "Why, when I have pulled all the right strings, has God not hopped to meet my desires?" They don't say it so bluntly, but that's the underlying feeling.

The need, then, is to pray for wisdom, seek good counsel, and obey all that we know to be God's will, yes. Maybe a leading will be confirmed by clearly providential circumstances or miraculous signs. More basic than all of these things, however, is our embracing God's values and centering our lives in God himself.

Now That I'm So Experienced

I believe I've learned a few things in recent years. I hope so; it would be a shame to go through what I have and not learn anything. As to guidance, I've asked myself the question especially relating to New Life USA, "Would I do it again?" Maybe not, and that bothers me. One of the great dangers of experience is that it gives the impression we can make wiser and better decisions just because we have it. That may be true sometimes but certainly not always. Experience can make us tentative and reserved, too analytical and even cynical. Experience claims credence simply because it exists, not because it has truly learned anything.

Experience can also pretend that the present situation is just like others that have gone before. The truth is I've had no experience of being the age I am now, no experience of functioning in the situation I am in now. I've never been this way before. I need God's guidance for here and now, rather than relying on "answers" I worked out in another time and for another place.

If I am not careful, experience can work against guidance. I must follow what I know to be the direction and voice of God, not because I have experience in what he is asking but simply because he is asking.

The mistakes of New Life USA concern me far less than the growing conservatism I find in myself, my tendency to analyze and to count costs that cannot yet be tabulated. I am not pleading for reckless nonsense now. I most certainly am not suggesting anyone should just grab "a word from the Lord" and plow ahead without careful planning.

I am simply arguing for a view of guidance that compels us in the face of human pain and need to say with the compassion of Christ, "I will do something." I am pleading for a guidance system that does not bow finally to the need to show financial profit or even fulfilled plans in order to validate success. I am asking that we judge whether an undertaking is God's will by something better and more biblical than the value system of Western materialism with its craving for more, bigger, richer. That something better and more biblical is the heartbeat of God himself.

Part 7

A Few Things I've Learned about Mystery, Faith, Truth, and Reality

15

About
Mystery

Have you ever asked God to let you know what was going on and have him just sort of stand there with his hands in his pockets? I certainly have. I like to refer to the absence of information in these situations as mysteries.

It's not really that God likes to be secretive. The problem is that we have an extremely limited frame of reference. We are so limited that we can't even grasp the nature of our limitations. We are very much like the five-year-old daughter of a friend of mine who startled her father one day by saying, "Daddy, I guess I know everything there is to know."

"Why do you think so?" her father asked.

"Well, I've thought and thought, and I can't think of anything I don't know!" she explained.

Like her, we have no idea how limited our understanding is because we can never compare what we know with the vast body of knowledge hid from us. Since we have no idea what we don't know, we can't get much perspective on what we do know.

Looking at the ways of God is a little like watching a parade through a knothole in the fence. We see an elephant, then a float, then just a part of a marching band. It's pretty hard to get the true picture of a parade that way. If we ever got a boost over the fence, we'd certainly see the parade far differently from before.

MYSTERY ISN'T MYTH

To say that mystery is inherent to our relationship as finite beings with an infinite God is not the same as saying we should abandon the use of our rational faculties and just try to experience God mindlessly in our spirits. To the contrary, Christ calls upon us to love God with all our mind as well as with heart and soul (see Matt. 22:37). In fact, one of the refreshing and unique traits of biblical faith is the absence of the mythological. The fantastic characters of Greek and Roman mythology are gone.

Jesus comes directly into the human scene as a human being. He is not protected nor does he shield himself from any human condition. Although he could turn stones to bread in order to feed himself, he will not. Although he could rely on angels to protect him in a dramatic leap from the pinnacle of the temple, he utterly rejects the idea.

Even around an astonishing event like the Resurrection, there is no magic, no trappings of mythology. Only a select few people are directly involved, and they are doubters, disappointed followers, and cynics. They are told to touch and observe; to examine evidence and satisfy themselves of the facts. There is no apparition, and nothing about the events that smacks of myth.

While there is no mythology, there is mystery. I can accept mystery with regard to faith because I am also surrounded by it in every other realm. I don't think it strange that God and his ways are beyond what he can explain to me because so much even of the physical universe is beyond me.

I have a friend who is a nuclear physicist. I said, "Will, tell me a little about quantum physics, just give me some kind of handle." He started talking and continued for about half an hour. When he finished, I looked at him and said, "What? What are you talking about?" He tried again and managed to break it down so that I could pick up some tiny bit of what quantum physics is. It's a whole science I hardly knew existed, much less understood.

One of the most frustrating periodicals I can read is a computer magazine. I may read a complete article and afterward not have the faintest idea what it said. It's not that I'm stupid; I just don't have the frame of reference to understand more than the elementary facts about computers.

I have had similar frustrations reading *Sky and Telescope* magazine. The past couple of years I have begun to get into astronomy with my oldest son, Jamie. We had been in the mountains camping. We looked up and saw all the stars, the same ones I had seen for fifty years, and I couldn't tell him one from another. I found the Big Dipper, and I thought I could identify the North Star, but that was it.

I decided I would never do that again. The next time we walked I would know something about the starry wonders over our heads. That started me on an incredible journey of discovery. I guess you could say it gave me another knothole through which to look at the parade. Really, one thing my study of astronomy does is give me some frame of reference to glimpse how much I *don't* know.

In many realms I live with mystery. I've mentioned quantum physics, computer science, and astronomy, but I would find the same mystery if I began looking into medicine, the mind, anatomy, chemistry, and all sorts of other fields. It should come as no surprise, then, that there is mystery also in the ways and works of God. In fact, all the other mysteries I mentioned *are* mysteries in the ways and works of God for He made it all. "Oh, the depth of the riches of the wisdom and knowledge of God! How unsearchable his judgments, and his paths beyond tracing out!" (Rom. 11:33).

LIVING WITH MYSTERY

Since we are not about to eliminate mystery from our faith or from the universe, we need to find ways to live with it. I want to suggest five ways:

1. *Find an answer when you can't find a solution.* We tend to think of answers as solutions, but we need to separate the two. Sometimes there are no solutions, but God will give us the answer we need to go on. Paul's thorn in the flesh is an example. Paul writes, "Three times I pleaded with the Lord to take it away from me. But he said to me, 'My grace is sufficient for you, for my power is made perfect in weakness'" (2 Cor. 12:8–9).

Perhaps the whole situation became less a mystery to Paul as time went on. He wrote that the thorn was given "to keep me from becoming conceited" (v. 7). It's not altogether clear at what point he figured that out, but it is clear that he didn't understand it at first or he wouldn't have prayed for the Lord to remove it.

Sometimes the best and only answer we can get from the Lord is, "My grace is sufficient for you." We may never find a solution; we may have to live with our problem— and our questions about it—until we get boosted up higher where we can see the whole parade from heaven's vantage point.

I think of Job as another person who got an answer but no solution. Unlike Paul who saw a reason for the thorn in his flesh, Job never did figure out what was going on. It's a fascinating story. The issue in Job is, "Why do people serve God?" Satan says, "They serve you because you are so good to them. If you would quit being good to them, they would quit serving you." God says, "Want to see?"

Job had everything go wrong that could go wrong, never had a clue as to why, but said, "Though he slay me, yet will I hope in him" (Job 13:15). At the end Job turns to God and says, "What was that all about?" God's reply did not deal with each of the questions Job asked, one by one. He did, however, come to Job in a way that answered the situation. He reaffirmed his love to Job, and in the end Job did have a new, firmer faith in God, although he did not fully understand. Certainly, if there had been in Job any element of serving God for what he could get, those wrong motives were gone.

In the next chapter, I will deal with a personal experience of my own that had a similar effect on me. I certainly am not Job, nor do I see his experience as normative since there was no one else in all the earth like him. I do, however, see the motive for serving God called into question at certain times for all of us. Expediency is an ever-present pollutant seeping into the best of our intentions.

It is important to note that Job was not reprimanded for asking his questions. Nor are we. There are, nonetheless, times when there simply is no explanation that can be understood from our perspective. I have discovered at those times a unique and precious presence of God. It is as though he, as my Father, crowds me closer to him in order to help me handle the mystery.

It is important, also, to understand how time can help us understand difficult circumstances. What at one point looks like total disaster may be viewed further down the road as a wonderful event. We must not put a period to a sentence where God has only a comma. God has a vantage point on the future that we do not have. Furthermore, he can be trusted with that future.

We must accept the fact that we cannot figure out God or predict his actions. His thoughts really are higher than our thoughts, and his ways past finding out. Yet because he is predictably good and constantly loving, we need never fear any of his thoughts nor shrink from his ways. When there is no solution, God himself is always our answer. This brings us to a second way we can live with mystery.

2. *Don't explain the unexplainable.* We live in a world where disasters and calamities happen, which is the nature of a world falling apart. Sometimes we get caught in the middle of it. What God has decided to do, despite all of that and even in the midst of it, is to give us eternal life. Even though we may sometimes seem to get caught in the cracks in this fallen and perishing world, it doesn't ultimately destroy us.

Often (and, I believe, more often than we know), God intervenes providentially to spare us from harm. I sometimes wonder how many things God has saved me from before they even happened. How many illnesses and accidents would have overtaken me apart from his providence?

When our oldest daughter, Carmen, was still small, probably ten or eleven years old, she was waiting to cross the busy street in front of our home. As she was about to step off into the road, she thought, "What would I do if an ambulance suddenly turned on its siren and came speeding down the street?" The thought caused her to hesitate, and in that moment an ambulance she had not seen turned on its lights and went speeding by in front of her, its siren screaming. Carmen is now a twenty-five-year-old mother of two boys. Yet we were talking about this event of deliverance in her life just the other day. It still says to her that God cares for her more than she knows.

Even when calamities do befall us, they cannot touch the eternal life we have in Christ. We are often so bound up in this present world that we tend to think when we are not comfortable here we have somehow gone wrong. We start raking ourselves, "What's wrong with me? God won't answer my prayer." We try to explain the unexplainable by attributing the fallout from a self-destructing world to our personal failings. The Bible is full of examples of the righteous suffering. It plainly tells us, "A righteous man may have many troubles" (Ps. 34:19), and "In this world you will have trouble" (John 16:33), but we somehow don't hear.

We insist on asking why. We want an explanation. We persist in trying to answer why for ourselves and others when as yet there is no answer. Earlier I said we could find an answer even when we can't find a solution. That answer, however, is not always an answer to why but often to who, an answer found in God himself.

Sometimes the unexplainable is something that does *not* happen rather than something that does. Two weeks before I went into the hospital with my heart attack, a woman came to me asking for prayer. She'd had an angiogram that showed two blocked arteries. She had been told that she needed open-heart surgery. She was scheduled for yet another angiogram and wanted prayer. So I prayed with her. She went back to the doctor for the second angiogram and her arteries were clear. It was a miracle.

Two weeks later on a Monday afternoon, I had a heart attack. A week later they did an angiogram and found I had three blocked arteries. I needed surgery. We prayed, of course, but no miracle came, and I had to have the operation.

I wasn't too happy with God. What is this? I pray for her and she's healed, but I have to undergo the surgery? I remember thinking, "God, did you mean to hit me with a miracle but missed and hit her instead?" God did just what you're doing now; he kind of laughed and said, "What I do with my miracles is my business." He chose not to heal my heart but to heal my life.

My view in retrospect is that God both saved my life and healed it. I had three diseased arteries. The smallest of the three was actually blocked, causing the least amount of damage. I am now enjoying a more healthy life over all than before, plus I was saved from what may very well have been an early death. I've listed elsewhere many of the other benefits I've received. All of these things were far from obvious at first; this is a good example of an answer I had to grow into. Today, I would not trade places with the woman who experienced the more dramatic divine intervention nor would I wish my route on her.

Have you ever felt that God got his signals crossed in dealing with you? You prayed for a job or a house or a companion or some money and then watched empty-handed as someone else got just what you requested. You felt like saying, "Hey, that was *my* answer. I was praying for $500, and she got it. God got the wrong address!" Be willing to live with some mystery. Don't blame God when things don't go as you think they should, but don't try to get God off the hook by blaming his inaction on somebody's lack of faith.

A lot of teaching these days says, "If you had enough faith, it would happen." Well how much faith does it take? How do you know when you have enough? The problem is you never know until it doesn't happen. Then you find out however much faith you thought you had, it wasn't enough. Then you face the same question again: how much faith is going to be enough? We treat faith like some inner barrel of water; it flows somehow into our lives but also leaks out, and we have trouble keeping the level high enough to score points with God.

Faith is not an inner barrel we must fill; faith looks away from ourselves to God for our answer. Jesus told the man born blind to go wash in the Pool of Siloam. "So the man went and washed, and came home seeing" (John 9:7). He showed faith by doing what Jesus said. Jesus told ten lepers to go show themselves to the priests. "And as they went, they were cleansed" (Luke 17:14). We could multiply examples like these. People showed by their actions that they had faith enough to receive God's answer.

Now someone tells us to place our hands on the televi-

sion as an expression of faith while he prays for our healing, or perhaps we are invited to come to an altar of
prayer. We lay our hands on the television or come to the
altar. If we are not healed, someone pipes up with the explanation, "You didn't have enough faith." Well, you had
enough faith to do what you were told to do just like the
man born blind and the ten lepers.

I don't know why God answers certain prayers and not
others. That's my point; we must not explain the unexplainable. We must be content to live with mystery. God is God,
and whatever he does is good. It will work out.

16

More about Mystery

I have suggested two ways to deal with mystery, with the unanswered and unanswerable questions we sometimes face in life. I said, first, that we can find an answer in God himself even when we may not be able to find a solution. I said, second, that we must be willing to live with some mystery, that we should not always insist on trying to explain the unexplainable. I want now to continue with four more concepts I've found helpful.

LET GOD SET THE AGENDA

Have you ever had the experience of trying to work on somebody when God wasn't? It's so frustrating! You see something in the life of another Christian, and you know it isn't pleasing to God. You want this person to change. So you pray for him, counsel him, and perhaps cajole him. You bind all the power of the enemy in Jesus' name. You enlist prayer from others. You pass along a book that has exactly what this person needs. The net result is zip.

Even if you succeed in getting the person worked up about his problem, you may simply produce confusion for him along with frustration for yourself. A fellow came to our senior pastor, Doug Murren, and said, "I've tried everything and just can't quit smoking. I've been prayed for, had it cast out, everything. I just cannot shake this habit; what am I going to do?" Doug said, "Well, just be the best smoking Christian you can be."

That's shocking isn't it? No, we have to accept God's agenda in other people's lives. Maybe the first thing God wants to deal with is not what you or I think he ought to. Maybe he is not nearly so concerned about someone's smoking habit as we are. Maybe somebody else's mouth, her talk, is not number one on God's agenda. These things may be high on our list. "If you're a Christian, you obviously don't do this or that." I know a lot of Christians who smoke. I doubt there will be ashtrays in heaven; whatever that habit fulfills will be fulfilled when we get there. Still, no one will go to heaven based on how many cigarettes they smoked or didn't smoke in the past year.

If you smoke, I imagine smoking will be on God's agenda at some point, if for no other reason than it's destroying your health. It will come up, and when it does, God will handle it. Between now and then, walk with confidence in God. Accept God's agenda for your own life and for others. You'll be a whole lot easier to live with.

Work where God is working; let him show you what he is doing. Wait until he invites you before you barge into others' lives to help God out. He may not need your help; he may be doing quite well by himself. But be open for business if he should want you in on the action.

ESTABLISH MEMORIALS

A fourth way to handle mystery is to record the mighty works of God that you witness along the way. Make a book of memorials in which you write down the great things God does for you. Has God ever done anything wonderful in your life? Write it down.

All through the Old Testament, Israel established memorials so that when they passed by the sites of their victories there was a historical marker. Their children would ask what the pile of rocks was for, and they would tell the story of what God did there.

Jacob set up a stone pillar to mark the place where he saw the ladder reaching into heaven and made his covenant with God (see Gen. 28:18). When Joshua led Israel across the Jordan, which God dried up at flood time, he had one man from each of the twelve tribes pick up a stone from the river bed. With these stones they built a memorial on the bank to mark the spot (see Josh. 4:1–9).

Israel created other kinds of memorials as well. They had songs that told stories. "We were in trouble with the armies of Egypt behind us, the sea in front of us, and we were dead meat. A wind came up overnight and when we awoke in the morning, there was a highway right through the sea. When we got through, the water swept back over the Egyptian army and we were free" (see Exodus 15).

Israel's great annual feasts were also memorials. At the establishment of the Passover, we read, "When you enter the land that the Lord will give you as he promised, observe this ceremony. And when your children ask you, 'What does this ceremony mean to you?' then tell them. 'It is the Passover sacrifice to the Lord, who passed over the houses of the Israelites in Egypt and spared our homes when he struck down the Egyptians'" (Exod. 12:25–27).

It's good to establish memorials. Where have you had a really rugged time but came through it better than when you went in? Write it down. It will be a help to you. Later when it seems your prayers are hitting a brass sky, you can go back to your book of memorials. The devil will tell you, "God never does anything for you. He never answers your prayers; he's like this all the time." Then open your book and say, "Ah, but that's not true. On such and such a date he did this, and there was the time he did that." You have it all down, and you can get excited just reading your book.

You can also create other types of memorials. A scar on
the ankle of our oldest son Jamie is a memorial for us.
When Jamie was about to be born, Barb and I had left the
house almost casually to go to the hospital. This was our
third baby, and we were veterans by now. We little imagined what an ordeal we faced. At the hospital, they took
Barb to the labor room and sent me to a waiting room. Back
then, fathers were treated as though they had nothing to
do with what was happening. Get them out of the way to
a room filled with jigsaw puzzles, checker games, six-
month-old magazines, and nervous, chain-smoking, non-
communicative men. Now everyone is invited in: dad,
grandparents from both sides, neighbors. You could almost
sell tickets.

I had settled down for a lengthy wait; the Cooks, for all
our experience, never were able to deliver very fast. In just
a few minutes a nurse burst into the room and called my
name. She said the doctor wanted to talk with Barb and
me together. Moments later he was explaining that he had
felt uneasy about the labor and decided to examine Barb.
In doing so, he had discovered a problem, and he needed
to do an emergency caesarean to deliver the baby. He gave
me a green gown and a mask and said I could stay with
Barb until the last minute.

We were both so shocked we didn't know how to react.
It all seemed like a dream to me, unreal. We had been
fortunate in our life together; other than the usual cuts and
bruises and dented fenders, we had never suffered anything. We had certainly never faced a crisis before. It was
hard to believe we were involved in one now.

As I remember it, I held Barb's hand and prayed a short
prayer. I told her I loved her and that everything would be
all right. People always say, "Everything'll be all right"
when they don't know what is going on and are worried.

During the delivery, I waited in the hallway as close to

the surgery doors as possible. Soon the doors burst open and out ran two green-clad figures, masks still in place, pushing a tiny baby in a mobile incubator. It was our son. They were taking him to the intensive care unit for newborns.

More time passed; I don't know how much. Things get blurry at such times. Again the surgery doors flew open and our doctor with other nurses and assistants came pushing Barb on a gurney. They rushed toward the elevator nodding to me to come along.

A short time later the doctor took me aside to explain the situation. Our baby, a boy, had been stressed during birth and had inhaled meconium, completely incapacitating his lungs. He was now on machines that might keep him alive. Those machines, we learned later, had just been purchased by the hospital and were the only ones in the city. Barb was also in difficulty, and they were having trouble stabilizing her blood pressure. He suggested I go to be with her right then and later go to the nursery.

When I reached Barb's side, she looked terrible. Not at all like the happy young mother I had brought in a few hours before. I took her hand and prayed with her. I stayed as long as they would let me and then went to the nursery. Our baby was barely visible behind the second window. There were wires and tubes everywhere. Machines were pumping and wheezing and beeping. Masked figures were clustered around the crib. How strange it seemed that all these people whom I had never met were working feverishly to save the life of my baby boy whom I had not even held. I had never felt more alone in my life.

I don't know how long I sat there, desolate. Sometime during the night I went back upstairs to be with Barb until they again asked me to leave. The doctor told me she was doing better and I should go home. He promised to call if there was any change.

I drove home in a daze. Once there, I sat on the edge of our bed nearly in a panic. Without even thinking I picked up a bedside Bible and absently thumbed through the pages. My eyes fell on these words: "Weeping may endure for a night, but joy cometh in the morning" (Ps. 30:5, KJV). It was like a personal message directly from heaven to me. I took hold of it, relaxed, and fell into an exhausted sleep.

I awoke to the ring of the telephone. The panic of the previous night returned, and I was afraid to answer the phone. Then I remembered the words, ". . . joy cometh in the morning." I picked up the phone and heard the doctor telling me that Barbara was doing fine and had been taken to a ward. The baby had survived the night. The doctor was very direct. "The machines are doing all of your baby's breathing. We don't know if he'll be able to breathe on his own after while. If he makes the first twenty-four hours, there might be hope."

Fourteen days later, Barb and I stopped at the bakery to pick up the cake we had special ordered for the nurses. On top were the words, "Thank you, from Jamie and his parents." We had come to know and love them in those two weeks as all of us had pulled together for Jamie. We were all smiles and a few tears as we took him home.

At the first doctor's appointment after Jamie's homecoming, we were shown three sets of x-rays. The first pictures of his lungs showed no capacity at all. They had been taken shortly after birth. The second x-rays were taken just before his release from the hospital. His lungs had obviously improved but showed serious scarring. The third x-rays were the ones taken just that day. They showed no scarring whatever. His lungs were normal. God had miraculously saved our child, but he had also used the gifts and ingenuity of our doctor. He told us later that Jamie was the sickest baby that hospital had ever saved.

The doctor was asked to write up his procedures. They had never been used before, but are today being used widely. Not only had Jamie been saved but hundreds of other babies as well.

Today, Jamie is a strong, healthy teenager. He has only one mark from his ordeal, a tiny scar on his right ankle. I'm not sure even how he got it. I do remember one of the nurses pointing out the small bandage on his foot. That scar is our memorial. When I noticed it I said to myself, "I'm not going to tell him what that scar is until he asks. Then, when he asks me what it is, I'll tell him the whole story."

When Jamie was about four years old, we had a little pool in our backyard and the kids were in it all day during the summer. One day Jamie came in and sat down and asked what the mark was on his foot. I said, "Let me tell you a story." After I'd told him the story he said, "Tell it to me again." Over the next months and years, I told that story five thousand times, it seemed. The other day he had his foot hanging out over the bed, and I noticed the scar. I pecked at it with my finger and said, "Remember this story?" We had a memorial of an act of God. It's wonderful.

CHECK YOUR FOCUS POINTS

When things aren't going as we'd like, when God's ways are shrouded in mystery, and if there's any plan behind it we haven't a clue as to what that plan is, it's easy to get our lives out of focus. We begin to inventory our debits, our lacks.

I've developed a list of eight focus points to help me at such times. I've touched on some of these points earlier, but here's the complete list:

1. Focus on who you are rather than who you are not.

2. Focus on what you have rather than what you lack.

3. Focus on what you know rather than what you doubt.

4. Focus on evidences of God's presence rather than apparent evidences of his absence.

5. Focus on health rather than pain.

6. Focus on your abilities rather than your limitations.

7. Focus on where you're going rather than where you have been (the future rather than the past).

8. Focus on God as the source of your life rather than random circumstance.

As with the memorials we talked about earlier, it's good to set down your focus points in a tangible form. What do you have going for you with regard to each of these eight points? Write down your assets, being as specific and also as comprehensive as you can be. If you do this, you'll discover that your present struggles and confusion can actually be a help to you in later difficult times. You can return to your list of assets the next time you get down. You'll begin to establish a pattern that will help keep your life in focus so that the unexplained and unexplainable things that happen won't be so likely to throw you for a loop.

SEE GOD AT WORK IN OTHERS

Sometimes it hurts to see God working in others' lives when we seem to be passed by. I told you about my dismay when God healed a heart patient I prayed for and then let me face surgery. Envy is always a possibility in situations like that. Instead of provoking envy, let God's work in the lives of others stimulate your hope. After all,

God is no respecter of persons. He is as willing to bless you as he is to bless that person who is at this moment in the most enviable position you can imagine.

The blessings coming to others are your evidence that God really is alive and well. He really is working; it's not the end of the story. Your turn will come. That's the way humanity is. "There is a time for everything, and a season for every activity under heaven" (Eccles. 3:1).

As Peter wrote to early Christians who had things pretty bleak, "After you have suffered a little while, [God] will himself restore you and make you strong, firm and steadfast" (1 Pet. 5:10).

Underneath it all, and however mysterious God's ways seem to you right now, please know that you're deeply loved by God at this moment. He has not forsaken you. He will never leave you. Maybe you're unable to understand what he is doing in your life; that's OK. He is working, and he will continue that work until the day you join him in glory. Then you no longer will see through a glass dimly and no longer will know only in part but will know fully, even as you are fully known.

17

About Faith, Truth, and Reality

Initial faith—the belief in Jesus Christ that brings us to know him as Savior—is the most elementary characteristic of Christianity. It's where we all start. It's how we enter the kingdom of God. Love, not faith, is the greatest element in Christianity (1 Cor. 13:13), but faith is what makes us Christians in the first place. It is also essential to living as a Christian, for "we live by faith, not by sight" (2 Cor. 5:7) and "without faith it is impossible to please God" (Heb. 11:6). Therefore faith is not only critically important, but it is something every real Christian already knows about firsthand, having entered the kingdom of God through faith.

Yet to know is not to know all. Most of us would probably admit that however long we have had faith and however strong our faith has been, we still have more to learn about it. I have been a Christian for many years. I have walked by faith and preached the word of faith, but I am still learning what faith is.

FAITH AND TRUTH, A MATCHED PAIR
Jesus said, "If you hold to my teaching, you are really my disciples. Then you will know the truth, and the truth will set you free" (John 8:31–32). Notice it is the truth that sets

us free, not faith. Unless our faith is based on truth, it can
bind us rather than free us. It can entangle us in all sorts of
strange webs, as I will detail shortly. More important than
believing, then, is believing the truth. The great healing
force in my life came from believing the truth of God's
presence. It did not come from believing my illness was
unreal.

When we have a biblical faith, we see God's presence
superimposed over all the other realities of life. That is to
say, we see life as it actually is, for God really is present
and in control. Our believing that God is present with us
does not make it true any more than not believing makes
him go away. Faith is not a means of getting God to be
present and thereby do our bidding. It is rather the means
by which we see that he is present. Thus, faith plus truth
equals reality.

An experience I had some years ago illustrates what I
mean. My dad and I, along with other family members,
were driving through a residential area in Seattle. Suddenly we saw smoke coming from one of the houses. At
first we thought it was coming from a chimney on a roof,
but as we looked more closely we saw that the house was
on fire. We stopped the car, and Dad went to a call box to
get help while I ran to the house to warn the people inside.

I rushed up on the porch and banged on the door. Then I
burst into the house and yelled to get someone's attention.
I found three people calmly sitting at the kitchen table
drinking coffee and visiting. They were shocked to see me
come running into the room. I told them that their house
was on fire and we needed to get things outside. They
didn't believe me and refused to move, getting quite upset
that I had charged in like that. Finally I persuaded the man
to come outside and see for himself. He got up grudgingly
and followed me out the front door. By then the smoke
was billowing out the upstairs windows and through the

roof. We ran back in and got the others and then started carrying out valuables as the fire trucks arrived, sirens screaming.

That episode illustrates how faith works with truth to bring us into reality. Their house was on fire; that was the truth. There was real danger, both to their lives and their belongings. The truth did not become reality to them, however, until they believed it, until one of them went outside and saw for himself. One look immediately changed his conclusions about his situation and about me. I was no longer some intruder playing a stupid joke. I was now a valued friend who had helped save their house and perhaps their lives.

Believing the truth leads us into reality. This in turn enables us to react appropriately, which can make all the difference in the world. The truth may shake us up. It may disturb our comfortable little coffee times, but it can also literally save our lives.

Faith and Untruth, A Mischievous Pair

Faith plus truth brings us to reality, including the ultimate reality, which is God. Faith does not create God or anything else. Believing does not make it so. Believing something that is not true brings us not into reality but into fantasy. So what do we have? Picture it this way:

> Faith plus truth equals reality.
> Faith plus untruth equals fantasy.

Fantasy can kill. The destructive force of faith based on untruth can be illustrated by my own experience with heart disease. Before my heart attack, I assumed I was healthy. I was doing all the things healthy people did. I was exercising regularly, watching what I ate, and getting adequate sleep.

When I was examined after the heart attack, the doctors discovered I had a cardiovascular disease. They said it was quite possible the disease had been active as long as five years without being detected. I was stunned. Just months before, I had gone with several friends on a float trip in Alaska. I went because I assumed it would be good for me, as well as great fun. Actually, it could have been fatal. We were in the wilds, far from any medical help or even communication. If I'd had a heart attack there, my chances of survival would have been slim. As I thought about my life over the preceding five years, I realized I had done many things I thought would be good for me when in reality they were harmful and could have proved fatal.

When we discovered the truth about my condition, almost too late, I was able to get help. I am now living in ways appropriate to my true condition. Living in fantasy about my health was pleasant for a while, but because it was untrue, it was harmful and could not continue.

When the truth is unpleasant, we have a strong tendency to deny it. Denial is so typical in heart attack victims that it's considered a symptom that can help diagnose the problem. When I took CPR training, our teacher made the point, "When a person has some chest discomfort but you aren't sure it's a heart problem, listen for denial. If the person is denying his situation or explaining it away, get him to the hospital as fast as you can. Heart attacks and denial almost always go together."

I don't think I am stretching it to say that life and denial almost always go together. We all cling tenaciously to our comfortable fantasies. A husband tells me his marriage is great, he loves his children, and he values his home. His wife tells me that he is never home, is prone to fits of temper, and she and the children are getting more and more afraid to live with him. A child, faced with the bad news of his report card, can't understand how the teacher could grade him so low. He has tried hard and done his work faithfully, he insists. The teacher, however, describes his behavior as disruptive and says he never does his homework. Alcoholics and drug addicts typically deny they are addicted. Others in their families may deny the problem too and become codependents, unable to help. Only when the husband, the child, the alcoholic, the drug addict, and their codependent family members face the truth and stop the denials will there be hope for positive change.

BELIEVING THE TRUTH ABOUT FAITH

We've talked about the necessity to believe the truth in any realm if we are to end up with reality. We must in the same way believe the truth about faith.

What is faith? What is it supposed to accomplish in our lives? The great faith chapter, Hebrews 11, says that faith was the secret of all the great people of God listed there. How does faith play a critical role in making us what God wants us to be? What is faith's dynamic, and how do we get from incipient faith to mature faith?

The development of a mature faith is sometimes not only a long process but a painful one. That may sound strange to those accustomed to thinking of strong faith as a *preventative* against pain, discomfort, and poverty.

I don't hold a preventative concept of faith, for a very simple reason: it isn't true. The life of faith is often painful, uncomfortable, and laced with deprivation. When our faith becomes an attempt to deny that fact, to create a different reality (which is really fantasy), tragic consequences can follow, as already explained.

Understand, I am not dismissing the power of the word of faith. It may indeed be possible many times to "name it and claim it." It is not altogether amiss to believe that, often, "what you say is what you get." But "getting" isn't the be all and end all of faith. If it were, Jesus could have but spoken the word of faith and the stones around him would have become bread. He perceived something Satanic in that suggestion and rejected it. He said, "Man does not live on bread alone, but on every word that comes from the mouth of God" (Matt. 4:4).

Jesus is the author and perfecter of our faith (see Heb. 12:2). The faith he has authored and works to perfect in us is not simply a means of getting things from God. Jesus didn't live by a "getting"-focused faith, and that's not what he wants for us. Mature faith is not measured by how effectively it gets things from God but by how it "sees" God in every circumstance.

A most difficult transition for me, and for many others with whom I have talked, has been to move from a *getting* faith to a faith that is also, and even primarily, a way of *seeing*. I believe this kind of vision is the hardest to obtain, but at the same time it's crucial for our faith.

CONSUMERIST FAITH INVADES THE CHURCH

There is little doubt that consumerism is a major characteristic of our day. We are a society of users. We seek, we consume, we discard. Our attention span is minuscule, our appetite insatiable, our loyalty nonexistent, and our lives fragmented. It occurs to me that when we focus on getting, we bring a similar consumer attitude to our faith. We employ faith to use God for our benefit, to turn stones to bread. We seek, we consume, and we discard over and over as our appetites demand yet another divine blessing. We want none of this patient, progressive Christian walk of endurance. Give us results right now, in an exciting fashion, and preferably with miraculous overtones.

As I said, I personally have not made the transition easily from consumer/user to companion, from a faith focused on getting to a faith focused on seeing God. I have not yet fully made it. My personal scales, however, are tipping more and more in that direction. As I look back, I think this transition began seriously when my faith formulas stopped working.

Consumerist faith, or faith as a means of getting, does tend to rely on formulas: "You do this and God will do that." Usually it works as we expect. At least, it does so often enough for people to get up and testify that, sure enough, they had faith and God rewarded them.

God doesn't always come through as advertised by those who purport to speak for him, however, so our "do this" lists tend to become longer and longer. We know that God cannot possibly fail, so if results aren't forthcoming, we must have missed something on our end. We add the something previously omitted and run the program again. After a while it becomes, "Do this and this and this, and God will do that."

Eventually the formula for getting becomes quite complex. If you pray this specific way, speak these particular words, refuse to believe any ideas or evidence to the contrary, keep paying tithes and giving offerings (more giving if you need more money), keep up with your religious duties (church attendance and involvement), never betray any bitterness or anger or unforgiveness, carefully maintain private devotions, act as if what you want is already there even if it's not, *then* you will get what you want from God. (And if that doesn't work, you can keep adding conditions.)

Paganism Invades the Church

Such thinking, although it is highly religious and sincerely heartfelt, is actually tainted by paganism. Of course, it differs from the paganism of primitive cultures in the objects and ceremonies of its ritual. Nevertheless, it is based on several wrong and basically pagan assumptions about God:

1. God is unhappy with me; therefore, I have to appease him.
2. God is reluctant to give me anything even if it's good; therefore, I have to coax him.
3. God is obligated to come through for me if I perform the proper ritual; therefore, I can manipulate him.
4. God is changeable and may alter his opinion of me at any time; therefore, I have to constantly prove I am a good person.
5. God is simply a responder and will react to me with either punishment or reward; therefore, I will do the things that will always call for a reward response.

Based on these false assumptions, we develop a set of rules and rituals that will keep God happy and generous with us. We do not sacrifice pigs, as the tribesmen do in New Guinea. We do not have spring fertility rites that will guarantee good harvests. We have other formulas and fool-proof methods, already described, for getting God to "move in our behalf." Most of these things are done in the name of faith, but changing the name and the ritual does not change essentially pagan attitudes into Christian faith.

In our section on the God revealed in Jesus Christ (pp. 33–37), I discussed this matter of what kind of God we worship and how that shapes us. We must reject all forms of paganism and the legalism that goes with it. Obligated relationships usually end up in alienation and bitterness. One or both parties will be disappointed because of unmet expectations. God relates to us not by obligation but by grace.

MY DISAPPOINTED EXPECTATIONS OF GOD

The last part of my life to come back together during the weeks of my retreat in Colorado was my faith. It wasn't that I had such a wrong view before. My understanding of faith had grown and progressed through the many years of pastoring and walking with people through the reality of life.

Nevertheless, I had become profoundly disappointed. I was disappointed with my frailty both physically and emotionally. It was taking so much longer to regain my strength than I had expected. Then, about the time I did start to regain my strength, I lost hold emotionally. For me, that emotional loss was harder at times than the heart attack. It was a weakness I hated and at times still find myself resenting when I refuse to heed the telltale signs that I am getting too tired.

Since I had such a "getting"-focused faith and God wasn't coming through for me, I must admit I was disappointed with God, too. All theology aside, it seemed to me God could have done *something* about all this. If he was not going to heal me of the disease directly, he could at least do something about the depression and emotional pain I was suffering. Actually, as I thought about it, why hadn't he done something earlier to alleviate the pressure that built to such crushing heights those last four or five years? I had faith in him! Why didn't he give me a break?

I guess, finally, I was disappointed in faith. Whatever it was, faith had not done a particularly good job in my life. Without question, much of this thinking was the depression talking. Depression does talk. It has its own reasoning just as an addiction does. It talks you right into its view of

reality and refuses to believe or even consider anything to
the contrary.

Be that as it may, while I was in Colorado, every time I
began to address these issues of challenge to my faith,
I became confused, frustrated, and anxious. I had little
choice but to put it on the shelf of my mind to be looked at
later. I knew it would have to happen, but in its own time.
I could not hurry it.

HE WAS THERE ALL THE TIME

One night I awakened after an hour of deep sleep. I felt
energized and couldn't go back to sleep. I pulled back the
curtains at my window and was awed by the beautiful
sight of new snow bathed in a brilliant full moon. I
dressed, put on my warmest sweaters and coat, pulled on
my boots and gloves, and stepped out the door. It was as
cold as it was beautiful. I started down the gravel road in
front of my chalet, the dry, powdery snow squeaking be-
neath my feet. As I write about it now, I am frustrated
because I cannot adequately describe the rare beauty of
that scene. It was breathtaking.

I walked briskly, my wool scarf pulled up around my
face. I had gone about half a mile when I heard the sound
of a jet passing overhead. I looked up to spot the plane,
but try as I might I couldn't see it. When you have been
alone for several weeks, as I had been, it doesn't take
much to capture your attention. I decided to take this
challenge: airplane, airplane, where is the airplane? I
played with the sound, trying to measure ahead to
where the plane should be; it was invisible. Then, suddenly, *God!*

I'm sure you would not have heard his voice had you
been standing there beside me. It wasn't a voice but a
knowing, a confronting. God was "speaking" to me. That
is not a phrase I am comfortable using. Even as I write it, it

bothers me, but I don't know any other way to explain
what was happening to me that night.

In looking for that plane, I had stumbled into God's presence, and he captivated me. I will verbalize what I knew
in an instant on the road. "Jerry, you can hear the sound of
that plane, and although you cannot see the plane itself,
you have no doubt as to its reality. You believe on the basis
of the evidence."

For the first time since my heart attack nearly eight
months before, I was able to think clearly, without
confusion about my faith. Now don't get the idea that I
had turned away from God, or was backslidden, or
apostate. There was no question whatever about my salvation. This was not about my salvation; it was about my
walk of faith with God. It was about a thousand unanswered questions, about doubts and disappointments that
in that moment seemed to loom higher than the towering
mountain peaks that stood behind me in rocky disinterest,
caring nothing for me or my faith.

In a much shorter time than it will take you to read
about it, all my hurts—the encased pain that even the
therapist and I working together had not been able to
touch—gushed out through my cries and tears as I sobbed
out my sorry state to this God who had interrupted my
walk. I remember thinking, "I should control myself."
Then, "For whose benefit? Why be controlled? Whose rule
says I should be?" I was sobbing out my guts, worrying
about who might be watching when there wasn't anyone
within a mile to see or hear or care. And in the freedom of
aloneness, I felt God.

It was not physical, as the voice had not been. Yet it was
stark presence. I don't know how long all of this took. It
certainly couldn't have taken long because it was extremely
cold out there. It was an encounter, an encounter that ini-
tiated faith at a different level, from a different base than

before. Not a faith hitched to God's willingness to perform, but a faith coming solely from the fact of his presence.

There came to me that night, not for the first time but in the most graphic way I had ever experienced, the stark reality of his presence with me. Not external, not "out there," but, yes, both "out there" and "in here." It was as though I were immersed in the Presence.

He gave me no instructions. He answered none of my questions. He demanded nothing from me. He explained away none of my doubts. What he did was show me that he had been with me through all the recent months of pain as well as the years before. He had been with me during the time of the church's growth. He had been with me through the times of difficulty and confusion and even bitterness.

This was no intellectual conclusion. I already "knew" he had always been with me because that is what my theology taught. But in my battle with pain and weakness, theological conclusions, even though I knew they were right, were not enough. They simply did not handle my doubts or answer my questions. Or heal my soul. But now I knew personally that God was there and had been there all the time.

WHEN GOD DOES NOTHING ABOUT OUR NEED

A good example of the "seeing faith" I am talking about is in the account of the time Jesus and his disciples were caught in a storm on the Sea of Galilee (see Mark 4:35–41). Jesus was asleep in the back of the boat when the storm came up. As it grew stronger, the disciples realized that this was more than a brief unpleasantness. This storm presented a major threat to their boat and even to their lives. They awakened Jesus and said, "Don't you care if we drown?"

Isn't it easy to conclude that because we can't see Jesus acting directly into our need, he is doing nothing? Like the disciples we wonder, "Doesn't he care?" Jesus so often responds in ways that surprise us. Seldom does he do what we expect. Here he gets up and commands the storm to stop. To the utter amazement of the disciples, the wind dies and the sea becomes completely calm. Jesus then asked them an important question. "Why are you so afraid? Do you still have no faith?" (v. 40).

Jesus clearly implied that something was amiss in their ability to assess their situation correctly and that there was a deficiency in their faith. Although they knew boats and storms and their own abilities, they had missed one important fact. Jesus had not come to die of drowning in the Sea of Galilee. He was not in jeopardy and, because they were with him, neither were they. Notice that their safety did not lie in what he was doing. It did not lie in their awakening him and somehow moving him to act. They were completely safe just because he was there. His presence changed the conclusions they should have reached about the situation.

It is the same with us. His presence changes the conclusions we should reach about our circumstances. Faith sees life through the fact of his presence. And his presence *is* a fact. He has said, "Never will I leave you; never will I forsake you" (see Heb. 13:5).

In my own case, God had not been waiting and watching to see how much faith I had before he finally decided to come to me. He was there all the time, but I was not able to see him. Just as the disciples had drawn wrong conclusions about their plight in the storm, I had drawn wrong conclusions about my circumstances. They were afraid they would go down with the boat and drown. I was drawing conclusions that made me doubt, have anxiety, and even feel bitter. He intercepted me, quite to my surprise, and helped me to see he had been there all along. When I looked at my circumstances through the fact of his presence, I saw the events in new ways. That is, I was able to see what is real.

BECAUSE GOD IS PRESENT

Someone has observed that our faith is the grid through which we interpret life. In this sense, everyone has some kind of faith. We all must use some viewpoint, philosophy, or belief system to explain life as it comes to us. Someone remarks, "That was a terrible thing." How has the person come to that conclusion? Through what grid is life being interpreted?

That night on that cold Colorado road I came to understand that my Christian faith is the *ability to interpret life through the fact of the presence of God.* As I said earlier, faith is a way of seeing. When I became aware of God's presence and began to interpret my life accordingly, it changed things. Several of the changes were:

1. *I no longer felt I was in such great danger.* A great storm had been sweeping over my life just as it had the disciples on the Sea of Galilee. Like them, I was beginning to wonder if I was going to make it. God didn't seem to be doing anything.

His presence changed all that because he has already conquered death and come out alive on the other side. It's not that he gave me courage to face death. It was much more than that. He gave me assurance that I shared his victory over death. He removed death's sting.

2. *My life once again made sense and had purpose.* It's not that he answered all my "why" questions. They were and are, for the most part, still unanswered, but in another way, they were totally resolved. He did not give an answer; he *is* the answer. I mean, when I saw him, I was able to rest with the fact that he has a total perspective on my

life and that it was under complete control. He is not just leaving things to chance, then waltzing in to give me theological clichés and divine slaps on the back to patronize me and make me feel better.

He is God. If he is present and controlling things, there is purpose. On that night I knew unmistakably, and still know it just as clearly: he was and is with me. I do not need to know the final sentence of my earthly story. I need only know that he will write it.

3. *I no longer felt like a helpless victim.* I had always been a person who needed to feel I was in control of things. Not that I could control everything that happened, of course, but I could handle whatever came. I had inner resources, alternatives, strength. All that had been swept away. Studies have shown that when an organism is placed in a situation where all its mechanisms for exercising control of its own life are removed, it leads to depression and even to a physiological deterioration of the immune system.

God's presence suddenly made me no longer a victim. I knew that neither disease nor depression would have the final say in my life; my heavenly Father would. It's just like a child's father showing up when some big bully has been shoving him around. The situation changes completely. Instead of feeling trapped and overwhelmed, the child feels secure and safe once again.

4. *I had hope for the future regardless of how dark the present seemed.* Because God is present, every ending for me is a new beginning. This is not a Pollyanna view that I use to insulate myself from the harshness of life. It is not pretending or wishful thinking. It is seeing life through the fact of his presence, which is the real way to see.

I remember the fear I had of returning home from those Colorado mountains. I had felt safe in a situation that demanded nothing from me. When Barbara came to drive home with me, I had such a flood of emotions. I wanted to go home. I had worked and prayed and ached for this day. At the same time, I wondered if the health I felt would be able to survive in the real world? When stress came, along with expectations, what would happen? What would I say to people who asked where I'd been? How could I describe, even to my family, what I had been through? Would they like me? I was very different now. How should I act? What should I say?

One thing gave me courage to pack and go home. It was the presence of the God of the night road. He was with me. Perhaps it was not accidental that this encounter had been saved until near the last. It was fresh in my heart as I started back to Oregon. I'm not sure I could have gone without it.

I was not mistaken about the fact that I would face difficulties after my return. It felt as though my life was ending not long afterward when I read my resignation to the church. But that wasn't all I felt. Underlying all the emotions was the realization, made indelible that night on the road, "He is with me. This may very well be a beginning and not an ending at all." Sure enough, it was!

Epilogue

The man seated in my office was in his late sixties, maybe even seventy. He was small and balding, with an open, exposed kind of face that looked intently at me. A few days earlier, his daughter had phoned me. "Dad is going to have open heart surgery and would really like to talk with you." Now, here he was.

"What would help you the most, George?" I asked.

He replied almost bashfully in a quiet but tense voice. "I want to see the scars," he said.

I really wasn't prepared for that request. I saw his anxious eyes fastened on the spot just below my throat where the top of the still-purple scar was visible with my open-collared shirt. I slowly unbuttoned my shirt. This was really strange!

George's eyes never left the scar. He took his finger and with an ever-so-slight tremble began to trace the mark.

"What are these?" He outlined the smaller scars on each side of the lower end of the incision.

His question brought back the terrible feeling of the tubes that had been inserted to clear the draining after surgery. "They put garden hoses inside your chest to take away the bleeding," I explained a bit indelicately.

"Can I see your legs? I understand they take veins for the by-pass out of your legs." Again his finger traced the scars on both my legs, ankle to knee. I was glad they had

207

used my lower veins rather than the upper. I'm not sure I would have dropped my pants even for this marvelous and frightened little man.

To my mind, my session with George that day symbolizes my long journey with you through the pages of this book. Just as I showed George my scars in hope of helping him, I have now, with the same hope, shown them to you.

This book has not been a discussion of further rules for becoming godly. I doubt that God himself could keep all the rules we have already invented to make us "good Christians." Frankly, my aim has not been to make you more religious. That is a direct route to guilt, condemnation, tension headaches, and anger. First, we become angry at ourselves, but ultimately we become angry with God. Long term, we simply cannot handle a deity who, in the name of love, wears us out emotionally, physically, and spiritually, but offers us eternity to get rested up.

If you still view the Christian life in that way, you haven't received the message of this book, and I can only hope you will read it again until you do.

I believe God wants to free you from the heavy yoke of religion. He wants to lead you into the glorious freedom that belongs to children of a loving heavenly Father. Personally, I have found this life of companionship with God to be truly liberating. My wife says I'm easier to live with now, too. Funny, I was thinking the same thing about her.

JERRY COOK is director of pastoral care at Eastside Church in Kirkland, Washington. A graduate of Fuller Theological Seminary, his previous publications include *Love, Acceptance, and Forgiveness* (with Stanley C. Baldwin) and *Choosing to Love* (with his wife, Barbara). He and Barbara are the parents of four and grandparents of two.

STANLEY C. BALDWIN is executive director of Stanley Baldwin Ministries, Inc. Drawing on his background in publishing and the pastorate, his many publications include *Take This Job and Love It, The Overflowing Life, When Death Means Life, Bruised But Not Broken,* and *What Did Jesus Say about That?* He and his wife, Marge, are the parents of five. They live in Oregon City, Oregon.